By K. Ross Toole

THE TIME HAS COME
MONTANA: AN UNCOMMON LAND

The Time Has Come

To Say the Things That Need to Be
Said About Campus Violence, the
Tyranny of a Minority, the Crusade
of the Spoiled Children, the Parental
Abdication of Responsibility, and the
Lack of Courage, Integrity, and Wisdom
on the Part of our Educational Leaders

by K. Ross Toole

William Morrow and Company, Inc., New York 1971

To Joan

Acknowledgments

I WISH to express my gratitude to Allan Toole, my cousin, and to Bruce Toole, my brother, both lawyers, who assisted me through the jungle of legal phraseology which had to be translated into English, and who gave advice and counsel. Thanks, too, to John Toole, another brother, who started the whole thing.

I wish to thank Arnon Gutfeld for stern criticisms from a young man's point of view, and my nephew, Howard Toole (who is twenty), for taking my hide off periodically.

I am grateful to my wife for infinite patience—and to my older children for good-humored tolerance.

Others with whom I have "rapped," young and old, I must thank collectively. There are simply too many of them to name.

Notwithstanding all this help, errors of omission, commission and interpretation are exclusively my own.

K. ROSS TOOLE
University of Montana
Missoula, Montana

Contents

To Whom It Ought
to Concern

THIS book is about the older generation (thirty to seventy), the younger generation (fifteen to twenty-four) and about hippies, yippies, violent campus rebels, revolutionaries, radicals, peaceful dissenters, commune livers, gurus, right-wingers, and silent majorities. So it is fair to ask at whom or what I aim to zero in on.

Well, obviously not at those under fifteen or those over seventy. Not because they aren't worth zeroing in on; they are. But not here. How about those between twenty-four and thirty? That age group has always had a certain ephemeral luxury of choice—and they have it now. They may take umbrage, be mildly annoyed, stirred or infuriated as they see fit to represent one group or the other—or themselves. Whatever their reaction, it is likely to be momentary because that is the nature of that peculiarly transitory age.

Historians (I am one by trade) in the drudgery of their training are constantly adjured, on pain of sudden separation from the graduate program, never to generalize and to be Olympian in their objectivity. They are told never to use weak

1

qualifying phrases such as "by and large," "in the main," "for the most part" and "in general." Of course, most good historians have recovered from such tenets and generalize when or where they please and, except for those whose specialized fields require quantification, most historians (who do much writing) qualify what and where it suits them with whatever choice of words appeals to them.

I intend to zero in on the "younger generation" and my own (I am fifty) without appending any glossary to define the terms I use. Admittedly, that is a risky business. When you use words such as "dissent," "liberal," "reactionary," "radical," "left" or "right" wing, or "revolutionary," there may be a wide margin left for interpretive error. However, if I fail to define these terms effectively in the context in which I use them, then what I say will be unclear. In that event, no one should bother reading beyond the first foggy obfuscation.

I have deliberately eschewed all but the most basic studies and polls which have presumed to pin down the nature and width (or narrowness) of the generation gap. I will make only fleeting references to the floods of material produced by "experts" aimed at analyzing, counting, explaining, defending, attacking, justifying or, in general, portraying why the generation called "the younger" is the way it is.

It is not that I have no respect for the authorities who have so abundantly flooded the market with studies on the subject; it is simply that this book is a personal statement based on observation and thought, subjective as well as objective. It is obvious, therefore, that I am influenced by the fact that I am fifty and not twenty. Quite as obviously I am influenced by everything I have done and been and become. I am a professor, but that is only relevant in the light of the fact that before becoming one (seven years ago) I was, among other things, a dude wrangler, a naval gunnery officer, an administrator (museums), a free-lance money raiser, and a cattle rancher. I have been married twice and in the aggregate have seven children ranging in age from nine to twenty-four.

Other "relevancies" as to why this book is what it is will emerge as I go along, but one in particular needs explication now. In the fall of 1969, as the result of several hours of conversation with my brother, who is fifty-four, I wrote him a letter which consisted, in effect, of an addendum to our discussion. In this letter I attacked what I considered to be the brutal and ignorant tyranny which a small minority of today's younger generation visit upon the vast majority of their own generation. I went on to condemn as naïve but dangerous the abuse and violence they heap not only on their own kind, but upon their elders. Some of the words were harsh ones. I called the violent campus rebels "slobs," said that they were "spoiled brats" and added that the greatest mistake my own generation had made was not the Vietnam War but was, rather, "its pusillanimous capitulation to its youth and its sick preoccupation with the problems, the mind, the psyche, and *raison d'être* of the young."

I said that what my own generation needed most was "not police, Mace, the National Guard, tear gas . . ." but "a re-appraisal of our own middle-class selves, our worth and our hard-won progress." And I concluded that we needed to use disdain and an expression of our disgust—and we needed to reassert our own hard-won prerogatives; that it was our country, too; we had fought for it, bled for it, that we loved it—and it was time to reclaim it.

My brother ran off a few copies for his friends on his Xerox machine. The friends ran off copies for friends, and with amazing rapidity, the "letter" was all over the state. It was quickly in the "public domain." One newspaper picked it up and then another. It spread from the *Boston Globe* to the *San Francisco Chronicle,* and then from the *Omaha Herald* to the *Hartford Times.* Within a matter of two months, more than five hundred newspapers, large and small, had printed it. Then it was reprinted in the *U.S. News and World Report* and then in the *Reader's Digest.*

The consequence of this rapid and, to me, utterly confounding spread of this short document was a deluge of letters from all over America and from dozens of foreign places. At first, beginning in about February, they came at the rate of a dozen or two a day. By June they were pouring in, as newspapers continued to reprint the piece, at the rate of two or three hundred a day. By July my wife, my family, neighbors and friends were still busy trying to open, read, and somehow to categorize some 20,000 letters.

This deluge, this phenomenon, the effort to absorb it and explain it, has a good deal to do with this book. I have no intention of dealing with the rough categories that emerged except to note that perhaps one percent were from the extreme right—cheering me on with rapacious glee—and one percent were from the far left bombarding me with epithets, the mildest of which was "fascist pig."

In the area between these extremes, there were gradations of approval, partial approval, rationally written rebuttals, comments, suggestions, and offers to go on the lecture circuit. But what impressed me most was that the *bulk* of the letters were from what I can only describe as very worried, often frightened, literate people, the majority over thirty, most of them college graduates—whose letters, often lengthy, expressed the deepest concern for the future of America in the light of today's violence and bitter dissent, particularly on American college campuses.

What matters in terms of this book, however, is that the deluge of mail, the thousands of commentaries, the overall expression of anger and frustration, forced me to ask basic questions of myself, my colleagues, my students, my children, my wife. I questioned lawyers, judges and farmers. I found the asking difficult, the answers unsatisfactory. But something began to jell in my mind and, I suppose, in my viscera.

What really happened, I expect, is that I listened more carefully than I had for years and delved into my own self more deeply than I had since I was an adolescent—looking backward hard and critically.

If I had suddenly seen the light—if this hard process of questioning and listening and remembering and thinking had resulted in some personal metamorphosis, I might, indeed, have written a book, but it would not be this one. I doubt that *reflection,* serious and concerted, very often results in inspiration. It may raise more questions than it answers. It rarely casts a bright, new beam into dark corners. But it does *something,* and part of that something is to trim some of the blubber from loose thought. It tends, too, to separate facts from opinions—which, somehow, in an unhealthy kind of symbiotic relationship, tend in today's world either to substitute for each other or to merge into each other as if they were not inherently different in aspect.

The fact that I am a historian has deeply colored my reflections. I remain skeptical of all-encompassing systems, instant solutions and of the ultimate efficacy of unleavened idealism. Nothing in my intense introspection of the past year, nor in the light of interminable new discussions with youthful antagonists and protagonists, has altered the fact that Santayana's aphorism remains valid: "A people who ignore history are condemned to repeat it."

It is the historian in me that refuses to yield the middle ground to either extreme and insists that one of the most deadly diseases of the intellect is dogma. The doctrinaire man frightens me; the ignorant man merely saddens me.

Mix up the words "fifty years of age" and "historian" and you are apt to find that there is another abiding conditioner: an abhorrence for the word "relevance" as it is so often used by the younger generation. This is not a Pavlovian reaction in defense of one's profession, it is a wincing at ignorance. The fact is that one man's relevance has never been another's and the further fact is that what is "relevant" today was not "relevant" yesterday and is extraordinarily unlikely to be "relevant" tomorrow. The word "now," so prominent in the lexicon of today's young, the emphasis placed, for instance, on the phrase the "now generation," is a first cousin to "relevance." It is anathema to sound thinking and to a pertinent dialogue because "now" is utterly fleeting. It is one fraction of a moment standing between the future and the present—it is a "feeling" which fails to take into account the enormous rapidity with which "now" becomes "then."

Most professional (i.e., academic) historians are "liberals." So am I. I will not belabor the word here. I will, I hope, define it critically and definitely enough in later context. It is worth mentioning here only because I will have few professional colleagues left across the country who will admit me to the camp once this work is published—in which event, insisting all along the way that I *am* a liberal, I shall find some other label under which to rest momentarily.

If I am drummed out of that particular corps, it will be

because, in the light of the past year's intensive introspection and extensive extrospection, I have come to a place, dead center, from which I need badly, for reasons of integrity and anger, to point a finger at the younger generation and at my own generation and say some extremely unpleasant things. I say "for reasons of integrity" advisedly. I think America is in trouble and in danger and I, as you, love this country. To see what I think I see and say nothing would mean being untrue to myself and it *does* follow as the night the day that if one is true to oneself "thou cans't not then be false to any man."

As for "anger," well, it arises from the fact that if we are brought down, it will not be because the savages surrounded us in the darkness of any night, nor by any creeping, foreign thing. It will simply be because the brightest and the best among us capitulated to myth, fear of ourselves, and of each other, and closed our eyes to the enormous strength and capacity we have at hand. And all that strength is there because we have been where we have been and done what we have done—but seem to have forgotten. We seem suddenly and foolishly to have forgotten. Having forgotten, we cannot tell the young where they came from or why they came, or where the wind tends.

That I will be accused of a frontal attack on a whole generation is a foregone conclusion. I do not intend, every time I refer to youth, to repeat *ad infinitum* that the vast majority of them are fine—in fact, probably more than passingly excellent. I will often say "entirely too many" or "a large proportion of" or "a considerable number of."

Al Capp once said, "I'm no more anti-student because I attack the SDS than *Life* magazine is anti-Italian because it attacks the Mafia." I am no more anti-young because I

attack a proportion of them than I am anti-American because
I deplore certain things going on in the country. Probably
the best distinction I can make here and now and early in
the game is to say to those under thirty who may read this
book—"If the shoe fits, wear it"—and let it go at that. If
I try to explain "a considerable number," or "entirely too
many," the process would be profitless and probably endless
and it would, in any event, be misleading. A very small number of young people with Molotov cocktails can be "entirely
too many." A relatively small, but vocal number of nonviolent
students whose view of America is dangerously warped can,
in effect, be a "considerable number."

William Morrow and Company recently published a book
called *Protest* edited by Julian Foster and Durward Long.
It is an excellent anthology of some 580 pages. In a section
by Foster, "What Is Known and What Is Said," the point
is effectively made that student protest is such a difficult and
ramified phenomenon that generalizations about it are almost
impossible. Perhaps. He goes on to say that analytical or
evaluative treatments such as appear in popular magazines
usually reflect a strong bias. True. I can only assert once
more that this is a personal statement, unscientific, originating
from personal sources, inner and outer, and that I present
it as such and nothing more.

It will be said (or it ought to be) that I teach at a small
(8,000 students) state university hidden in the fastnesses of
Montana's mountains, that our campus has been relatively
calm and that thus removed from the storm center of things
I can only write of these matters from second, third or even
more remote sources. That, as it happens, is nonsense. The
academic world is a small one and like most of my kind
I am peripatetic. I have recently returned from trips to both

coasts, visiting, listening, and watching, from Harvard to the University of Washington. Moreover, I am concerned not only with students per se but with the young. I have a sort of menagerie (my own progeny and their friends and the progeny of my friends' friends) under my nose most of the time.

I shall do very little in this book with black activists, the Black Student Union and other on-campus black organizations. This is the case because I believe that the black militant differs inherently from the white. The black militant is, it seems to me, a pragmatist, rhetoric notwithstanding. He does not want to destroy "society," he wants in it, and he wants a larger share of its largess. On campus his demands are usually for a larger quota of blacks vis-à-vis whites—or an insistence on stronger and larger black studies programs. He tends, also, to make an issue over the number of blacks employed on university construction programs. Though militant whites have sought again and again to make common cause with blacks, their alliances have been tenuous to say the least. The black has a deep suspicion (thoroughly justified, in my mind) of the white militant and tends to go his own way in his own cause.

Two things I should assert now so that I need not assert them with monotonous iteration in the text. In defending my own generation, which I consider to have been and to be a most remarkable and productive one, I do not mean to imply that there is nothing wrong with America today. There is a great deal wrong and if we are going to preserve the Republic, many ills must be cured. I will, I hope, make it abundantly clear in the text that I think the ills are curable—and without violence or revolution.

No matter how often I assert the contrary, I shall be accused of advocating suppressive techniques which are anathema to the Bill of Rights and constitute a diminution of civil and constitutional rights in the name of order.

I advocate no such thing. Dissent, peaceful protest, the right of the individual to his privacy are vital to the functioning of our system. It has taken us years of travail to bring "due process" to its present state of development. I do not advocate that we depart from the tenets and imperatives involved in "due process" in any way. To do so would be self-defeating and tragic.

It may be unseemly to bite the hand that feeds one, but I am at least going to nibble on it. One of the things that has happened to me in the past year of travel, interviewing, letter reading, reading, listening and hard thought (and it has happened again and again in some strangely quiet and peculiarly unused portion of my mind, first as a whisper and then as an insistent cry) is this: My God, at the core, what a vast number of the youth are saying is right. Twist and turn as I might, attack them where I will, at the heart of many matters of great moment to them, to us and to America, they are right.

And so, mid-discourse, as it were, having attacked their generation hotly and defended my own with fulsome righteousness, I shall turn about and attack my own generation.

Emerson is usually quoted as having said, "Consistency is the hobgoblin of little minds." What he really said is that "foolish" consistency is the "hobgoblin." This, then, in my method of attack, defense and attack, is an inconsistent book. All I can hope is that that inconsistency is not "foolish." These are, after all, inconsistent times, filled with issues and problems which are, within themselves, inconsistent. There is inconsistency in the views which both the older and the younger generation take.

After watching, talking, listening and thinking about all this I feel no sense of despair. All around me in America I see problems and harbingers of deeper problems. But in both the young, the middle-aged and the old, I sense great resiliency, adaptability and strength—if only these qualities are not negated by jejune anarchism—if only we ourselves do not short-circuit the system which promises to keep us in the rational middle. For there and there alone we will solve what is solvable.

Chapter 1

Of Age, Time, and of Generations Gapping

THE younger generation in America has much to commend it. I doubt that it has more than, say, the generations born circa 1800 or 1920, and I doubt that it has more per capita intelligence or perception than most other American generations. It has, clearly, more information, because it has greater sources and resources from which information, per se, arises. Those sources and resources, incidentally, were devised by my generation. Television, the computer, information retrieval systems, microfilm, mechanical teaching aids and machines were all products of my generation, not theirs.

The fact remains that they have more information on a worldwide basis than any preceding generation. It does not follow that they are either more sensitive or perceptive because of this informational explosion. That remains very much to be seen. That they live with more awareness of what goes on in the world than did preceding generations is patently obvious. That this lends itself to a certain discomfort and confusion is also obvious, as is the fact that the same discomfort afflicts everyone—regardless of age or education.

The massacre at Mylai comes into the living room via the tube and raises the same grim specter for old and young alike. The riots and beatings, the gatherings and murmurings, the absurdities and cynicisms which are age-old (but were once hidden in their separate compartments far away) now peep or glare or pour into every living room. Man has not changed. But the ways in which he can see himself in action have changed enormously and quickly.

That this has resulted in painful reappraisal of reappraisals is perfectly evident. That it has led youth into a hard view of mankind and a deep concern for the future is just as evident. That the discomfort, the pain, the reappraisal is the exclusive property of youth is absurd. Indeed, it might well be argued that youth, whose roots are more shallowly spread in past traditions and old views, can and should be less upset than their elders. They have not, after all, undergone radical surgery on fondly held and long-standing verities. They are, therefore, less vulnerable, less easily wounded, or should be.

Yet a great many of them, a percentage significant enough to have attracted the almost incessant attention of "the media," hours of prime time television, pages by the thousands in *Life, Look, Harper's, et al.,* and in the movies, books, plays, and recordings, have emerged onto this rapidly changing scene as full-blown cynics, convinced that America is rotten to the core and that all old values are fake, hypocritical, crass and destructive.

While it is true that the media tend to focus on what is bizarre and incline to cover the momentary action of the few rather than the long-pull quietude of the many, even so, a *significant proportion* of the younger generation has fallen down before the wind blew, has substituted "gut reaction" for reason, has confused fact with opinion, has "dropped out" or "turned off." Why?

The reasons they themselves give, repeated from a thousand platforms at a thousand rallies, in a thousand essays from a thousand outlets for three thousand six hundred and fifty days, have, all together, become a monotonous litany of despair. Technology has destroyed the quality of life. Man has been dehumanized by war, hardened into vicious callousness by the acceptance of violence as a way of life. The pursuit of material things has withered the soul of America. "Society" has calcified into a rigid structure held together by racism, capitalism, the military-industrial complex and an immoral government. The older generation has left them a heritage of hate and ignorance and bigotry. It has left them an ecosystem on the verge of cataclysmic disintegration. The "establishment" is insensate, corrupt, greedy and blind. It forces all Americans to march, lockstep, automatons, toward a future without love or joy—off toward perpetual immoral war. Change is impossible because the wealth and the power of the country are concentrated in the hands of a few warmongering, evil men bent on profit. The answer? On the one hand, "to the barricades"—on the other, "to the commune." In either event, these young Americans, usually vigorous and bright, are lost to the country at a time when we need them badly.

Is what they say true? There is truth in it. Is it an accurate view for the most part? It is an absurdly oversimplified, grossly naïve, ignorantly fragmented, rigidly doctrinaire, blindly intolerant, righteously distorted picture of America. Then why do they say it and how can they believe it?

Precisely, I think, because they have been unable to put together the facts which have been poured in upon them by the explosion of new, instantaneous and intimate sources of information. Precisely because television, data-processing, and documentary film techniques bombard them with events happening simultaneously the world around—but they have no context in which to place these events. They have no perspective, no promontory from which to view these events and this information. In short, they have no rudder.

It is not so much that they view as through a glass, darkly. It is that they view incompletely, accepting pieces as wholes—or, rather, putting pieces together to form wholes, ignoring the fact that when they have finished putting the puzzle together, they have half the pieces left over. They present to each other and to my generation—and to the world—the picture of America thus arrived at—their own portrait of Dorian Gray, incomplete, warped, inconsistent with root facts—but at least it is their own. Perhaps it is that latter fact that gives rise to the righteousness with which they defend absurdities.

They have an advantage, too, these, the militants, the despairers, the commune dwellers, the "turned off." Their advantage lies in the fact that there *is* so much wrong in America; there *is* so great a need for change, for reclamation, for new ways to deal with old problems. So their appeal extends beyond themselves to others who know that all is not well and who, when the mob gathers to burn the ROTC building, do not run for the fire hose, but stand there confused. Maybe, after all, these violent ones are right. So a considerable mass does nothing because it is not sure. It stands there or turns away—and goes home. Maybe, just maybe, America can't change. And a great many wait to see. They are quiet, but waiting to see. They have faith on Monday that they lose on Tuesday and regain on Wednesday. Indeed, the younger generation in America has much to commend it—how much will depend on which way it turns when the time comes. When the time comes? What time?

Well let me address myself primarily now to you, the waiters, the uncommitted, the young doubters—because the way time will come will be FAST.

Time is supposed to flow along evenly. The calendar says so, the clocks say so, and the sundials have said so for many thousands of years. Throughout all of those thousands of years, the young, because they are young, have believed that time comes evenly out of some inexhaustible reservoir. The young know that they are mortal in their minds, but they do not know it in their hearts. There is plenty of time. The options are myriad. You begin in a great curved room with a hundred doors. You may choose any door. Choose one and there is another room, wonderfully beautiful, with many, many doors. And you may open any door. Choose one and move on. Everything is new and beautiful. The room is slightly smaller and the doors are slightly fewer, but there are still many choices.

So it is that there are an infinite number of girls you may one day love and marry; so it is that you may one day be a locomotive engineer, a pilot, an artist, a dancer, a writer. Ultimate choices are far, far away, through many doors and beautiful rooms. Sometimes you go back through the door whence you came in and try another door—again into a slightly smaller room with slightly fewer doors.

But the fact is that time does not flow evenly and inexhaustibly along. It accelerates. Its appetite is voracious and it feeds on your options. They dwindle. The rooms shrink, the doors grow fewer and fewer. The infinite number of girls you might love and marry become one. The things you might have been become one—and that is what you are. Every door through which you pass loses you the doors through which you might have passed. Time pushes you along, forces your choices, eats up your chances.

For a long time you do not have to decide what shall weigh heavy and what shall weigh light in your life. You may choose city or country, action or inaction; you may decide on money and things or family and fewer things—or nothing at all.

For a while you have alternatives with your children; you may choose permissiveness, close regulation, a mixture. You may experiment, being a buddy rather than a figure in authority. There are many doors. But then, with startling speed, the effects of the course you have chosen manifest themselves in the child. And then your alternatives are gone. You must then do what is best for the child as you see it in the hard light of cause and effect. The doors behind you are closed.

In all this, as you go along, there is a sense of loss—the loss of the other choices you could have made but didn't; the wrong choice you made but couldn't find your way back through the door you had mistakenly chosen. There is a sense of loss, too, in the almost always belated recognition that a year at twenty is three years long; a year at sixty is six months long.

The point is that with time devouring your choices you cannot have the whole world, all the beautiful rooms. You cannot go through all the doors. Sometimes you can retrace, but not often. You cannot avoid mistaken choices and you cannot stay in one room. Time will not let you. You cannot drift.

Is there a plan in this labyrinth? Is there a map so that you might open all the right doors at the right times? Most assuredly not. Because this is a process, not a place, and because the last door is death. Because the choices are, in fact, the process of maturing—all the choices, all the doors. No man or woman living or dead went through the labyrinth without pain. The price of maturing is pain.

So you are waiting to see about America? You are waiting to see if the country can change without spilling ten million gallons of blood and burning down its cities. And you are looking around you at all the inequities and injustices—at pain and poverty. And you are waiting. But you will have to move on, very soon, opening doors.

As you wait and listen to the rhetoric from the bullhorn, listen very carefully. As you visit the commune and rap with its dwellers, listen very carefully. Because the words they are using are not what they mean. It is not in the clichés and the cadences. It is not in the statistics. What they are saying to you is this:

Look, man, you can have *all* the beautiful rooms. Don't grow up; don't move on; don't make hard choices. Open no doors. You are entitled to all the beautiful rooms, *now*. It is simply a matter of "life style." Don't pay. There is no excuse for pain. Joy and love all the time in all the beautiful rooms, *now*. Only first, man, we have to tear down the system that makes us pay. We have to tear it down or turn our backs on it. These choices, these doors, they are designed by the establishment to make you pay. Join us, stay with us. No pain, no payment, no hurt—just all the beautiful rooms, now. Look, man, don't grow up.

Why have the militant young no perspective? Why have they no promontory from which to look out over things? Why no rudder? It begins, I think, with the simple fact that they are young and hence see only in one direction rather than in two. They have very short personal pasts—so there is built-in imbalance in their view of things. But, one may ask, has that not always been true of all generations? The answer is a qualified "no."

Today, slightly over 50 percent of college-age students enter college—thus postponing the rapidly maturing process of work, marriage, children and responsibility at an early age. This percentage has steadily increased since the Civil War, when, as a matter of fact, education beyond grammar school was the exception rather than the rule. At the turn of the century roughly 5 percent of those of college age went to college. We have thus created a post-adolescent period in the lives of some 7,000,000 young men and women. And their maturity in terms of experience and responsibility, as opposed to information, is thus delayed.

In the capacity to *see,* to understand, to tolerate what must be tolerated, experience is a far more active catalyst than formal learning. At the same time that we have created this hiatus in the development of young men and women, we have created the information explosion—and subjected these students to enormous doses of new and often frightening facts about mankind and his potential—facts that, without mature thought processes, without the leavening influence of personal experience, without the benefit of personal hindsight, can easily be misinterpreted as harbingers of cataclysm and Armageddon. These facts, this abundance of new information, burst upon a percentage of the younger generation who have no personal philosophy—and hence no rudder.

If this is even a partially valid analysis of the militant's view, why does that view, that despairing, violent, blind lashing-out not affect *all* of the younger generation in our colleges? To some small degree it does, but the vast majority are *not* radical, not despairing of the "system," not commune dwellers and they have condemned and eschewed revolution and anarchy by the millions. Why? I suppose that the reasons are innumerable.

In the first place, in any given large conglomeration of human beings, there will be a small percentage more volatile, more aberrant, more unbalanced than the others. In the second place, though the age is permissive and from Dewey to Spock has been marked by a kind of relentless retreat from rudimentary discipline, a great many parents, either instinctively or as the result of unsatisfactory early experiences with permissiveness, have simply refused to go along and have worked hard and intelligently at setting forth behavioral guidelines that constitute a philosophy. They have inculcated in their children for eighteen years a sense of responsibility, civility, respect for democratic processes.

While the churches, too, have become permissive and are, indeed, torn within themselves by strife and disagreement, a percentage of the college generation has nonetheless received religious training which mitigates against the radicals' essential appeal to despair and destruction.

The college campus itself, especially the multiversity, has changed drastically in the past decade or so. It has had to. In the light of sheer numbers it cannot stand *in loco parentis* as once it did. So it, too, has relaxed regulations and, again due to the weight of numbers, a gulf has thus developed between faculty and students and administration. This is the fieriest kind of fuel for the violent radical. It is profoundly disturbing to the earnest nonviolent student. But it is a fact of life and it is very unlikely to change much. It is one of the doors that were opened—and the college generation will simply have to do what it can with the consequences.

Make no mistake, however, that the "action" *is* on the college campus and that it will remain there for a long time. It is important for my generation to understand why. Unfortunately, that requires at least momentary consideration of "the Generation Gap," per se.

Abundant sociological and psychological studies have been made of this phenomenon. Only a few of the conclusions reached by the experts need concern us, but they are germane.

Admittedly the Generation Gap is one of those terms that imply an all-inclusive set of conditions and circumstances. It suffers from abysmal overuse as a phrase and, as far as the majority of Americans are concerned, its existence in all realms of thought and activity is pronounced and positive. Yet there is much evidence that such is simply not the case.

One meticulous study of students enrolled in three Southern California colleges revealed that of the total number of students interviewed, 80 percent reported close rapport with their parents, and only 20 percent indicated *any* kind of breach, with a very small percentage indicating fundamental disagreement on basic matters.

Similar findings arose from Samuel Lubell's studies. Lubell reported that only about 10 percent of the college youths he studied revealed serious discord with their parents—and among these 10 percent, most involved long pre-college histories of family tensions. Many studies have concluded that the militant, alienated college student's troubles surfaced long before the college years.

Is youth *in general* radical in politics or militantly liberal? The University of Michigan made an in-depth study of the politics of youth, college and non-college, in 1968 based on the election of that year. These facts emerged: the under-thirty voter was clearly and positively over-represented in the Wallace vote—and not only in the South, but outside that area. The study, which was massive and careful, revealed that about 75 percent of the under-thirty voters voted the same party as their parents did.

Other similar studies make it clear that *politically*, the rebellious, radical youth were the products of liberal-left parents. In terms of *values*, traditional convictions, new moral and ideological concepts, studies have shown that as many as 80 percent of young Americans tend to be traditionalists.

But, since we are concerned for the moment with campus reflections, it is important to note that studies also reveal rather conclusively a greater "gap" in all areas between non-college and college students—a greater intra-generational gap than inter-generational.[1] What the studies do *not* point out is that that gap could be of enormous significance. However obnoxious the word may be, the 7,000,000-odd college students do constitute an elite. They will fill the highest posts in government; they will become the editors, the "opinion makers," the movie directors, the writers of books, the teachers and professors.

So while the generation gap as a sharp and decisive cleavage between old and young should be taken with bundles of qualifications and a pound of salt—so should the studies that presume to reveal that there really isn't any such thing. There clearly is, intra and inter. Quantification, which is involved in all these studies, leaves one distressing question not only unanswered, but unconsidered. It is superficially impressive to ascertain that 80 percent of the young are "traditionalists." But that leaves 20 percent unaccounted for except

---

[1] For a good review of and commentary on these studies see Joseph Adelson, "What Generation Gap?" *The New York Times Magazine,* January 18, 1970.

for the implication that a high percentage of that 20 percent is concentrated on college campuses.

The American university or college is perhaps the most vulnerable institution in the country. What percentage of its students is required to burn it to the ground? Especially with the "middle-of-the-roader" standing impotently by, how many militant, violence-prone students does it take to stop the machinery of the institution completely? If the experience of the past seven or eight years means nothing to the quantifiers, it had better mean something to the rest of us—because the simple fact is that it takes a very, very small group of students indeed to bring a great university to its knees, to change its curriculum drastically and foolishly, or simply to shut it down. That the majority of students are not involved in no way alters the consequences, which are both immediate and long-range and in both respects they are grave.

Schools that have undergone repeated violence and disruptions are characterized by an exodus of the best faculty—and it takes years, often decades, to build a good faculty. It can be lost in a year or two. There is a deceptive character to this loss. The best faculty members are the most mobile. Even in a tight market—which presently exists in practically all disciplines—they are constantly being bid for by other institutions. Most of them have tenure. They do not simply quit the beleaguered institution en masse; they take their time, fulfill their contracts, wait for the best offer and then leave. The process can be almost imperceptible. It is also inexorable.

Similarly, the besieged school can recruit only with great difficulty. It cannot get the best men at all, and even the mediocre, or worse, are reluctant, in spite of pay increases, to move into situations where teaching is difficult, morale is low and the faculty intimidated.

The more immediate effect may be even more devastating, especially for state institutions. For a decade now, a growing public wrath has been directed toward the students, faculty and administration of institutions where violence has occurred. It takes no poll to recognize that the anger is there and that it is wide and deep. Of the thousands and thousands of letters that I have received in the past seven months, it is a rare one that does not, in one form or another, exhibit some form of anger—ranging from chronic indignation to outright fury. These angry people are not interested in fine distinctions; they are not interested in percentages, nor in convoluted explanations of the nuances of academic freedom. They are furious over smashed computers bought with hard-earned tax money, they are indignant about the damage to public property; they are deeply angered by what they consider to be faculty incitement of students and administrative timidity.

This anger, indeed, has spilled over onto institutions where the peace has been kept and disruptions have not occurred. It is nationwide and probably endemic.

No legislature can ignore it, nor can regents, boards of education, or other constituted governing bodies. These bodies hold not only the purse strings but the power to control and regulate conduct, student and faculty. In the past few years, in many legislatures and on many boards of regents, a few cool heads have often prevailed and the institution in question has survived with its essential structures and freedoms intact. But nobody, elected or appointed, responsible in the end to a constituency, can indefinitely circumvent that constituency's demands. Those demands are today more insistent, more strident, more angry than they have ever been before in the history of the country.

So the minority on the campus brings down on the heads of the majority not only the hot ashes of burning buildings, but in all likelihood it will bring about the shattering of that peculiar and necessary immunity that the institutions of higher learning have to have if they are to function as they must. The minority can, in other words, destroy academic freedom.

When I pointed all these consequences out to an SDS activist a short while ago, he nodded in vehement agreement. "Precisely," he said. "We have to destroy that freedom in order to acquire a larger freedom—just as we must use guns to end the use of guns."

The American university is a fragile institution indeed. This student knows that. All the activists know it. But a great many people do not.

Chapter 2

A Fragile Thing, The University

A FEW years ago, John Masefield, England's poet laureate, wrote of British universities (and, for that matter, of all universities):

> There are few earthly things more beautiful than a university. It is a place where those who hate ignorance may strive to know, where those who perceive truth may strive to make others see; where seekers and learners alike, banded together in the search for knowledge, will honour thought in all its finer ways, will welcome thinkers in distress or in exile, will uphold ever the dignity of thought and learning and *will exact standards in these things* [italics mine].

That description could be applied to very few universities today not only because Masefield's lyricism leads to a picture of the ideal as the actual, but because, in many respects, today's university is seriously flawed. Part of its vulnerability lies in the fairly recent (since World War II) compact it has made with government—and with the unpleasant consequences of that compact. It *is* open to the charge that it has narrowed its function, participated in an emphasis on pragmatic research at the expense of the pursuit of knowledge for knowledge's sake—and become a kind of fourth arm of government.

In "The Deviant University," an article in *The University Bookman*,[1] Donald Marquand Dozer takes off on the faults of today's university, pointing out that it has been a crashing error for the university so thoroughly to identify itself with "public authority." For many years, says Dozer (a historian, incidentally), "The university has been alienating itself from the kind of world these young rebels intuitively aspire to see and live in." And after chronicling a generation's change in university philosophy and policy, Dozer concludes that "the university must reclaim its traditional role as a sublimating influence in society, upholding ideals of the true, the noble, and the beautiful. It should begin again to vindicate the ideals of education, *which, as it happens, are also the ideals of youth* [italics mine]."

There is much merit in Dozer's attack on the faults of today's university. There is little to buttress his assertion that the "ideal" university could, should or ever has been a reflection of the ideals of youth. Indeed, one of the classic functions of the university has been to leaven untrammeled youthful idealism with large doses of hard fact, a skeptical study of man's past, a cautious appraisal of his limitations and a hard look at the world he lives in and will have to live in.

Literature on campus crises is heavily burdened with this attitude: "After all, the kids are right, even though they may not know why. It is basically the university's fault that all this is happening to us." Most of this literature emanates from

---

[1] Donald Marquand Dozer, "The Deviant University," *The University Bookman*, Autumn, 1969.

professors or university administrators—and most of it is simply poppycock.

Of course the universities are troubled. In view of the enormous inundation of students for which they were ill prepared; in view of turmoil, ideologically and practically, swirling around America; in view of inflation, withering budgets and the slings and arrows fired by that small but potent group of Americans who have always been anti-intellectual; in view of rapid, indeed, explosive social, economic and political changes in the span of a few short years; in view of technological advances of breathtaking magnitude, *what institution geared to learning would not be in trouble?*

I do not believe that any educator can consider any university's curriculum as of 1960 and compare it with the curriculum of 1970 without coming to the conclusion that the institution has striven mightily and in many respects successfully to change in the face of the need for change. And this, I am confident, is true of the vast majority of American universities and colleges. Curriculum is one of the hearts of the matter.

I do not see how any educator, unless his parochialism is overwhelming, can deny that every institution of higher learning worthy of the name in America has spent at least the last seven years scrutinizing, reevaluating and rethinking the university's role vis-à-vis government, government contracts, and government-sponsored research. *Most* universities have formulated strict policy governing this activity and many have completely severed all connection with any government agency which calls for even the slightest alteration of the institution's formally stated educational philosophy.

The internal critics of today's university should step back

from the trees at least far enough to get a glimpse of the forest. They should recognize that there is very limited efficacy in self-flagellation. Even though their own discipline is not history, they should look backward from where they are and try for a little perspective. All is most certainly not well. There is much need for further change. But the average university is meeting the challenge admirably.

The student may sometimes, at least, be excused for confusing "now" with "always has been" and "probably always will be"—but there is no excuse for a presumably mature faculty member viewing an enormously swiftly changing scene as a static scene.

What of the lay critic of the university? First of all, today they are legion. "Town and gown" conflict is nothing new and lay criticism of institutions of higher learning has waxed and waned since 1209 when Oxford University moved itself lock, stock and library from Oxford to Cambridge when the city fathers and the University had a falling out. For obvious reasons, lay criticism tends to be directed at liberal arts schools rather than agricultural, medical, law and other "trade-oriented" enterprises.

Today's lay criticism is overwhelmingly rooted in a disgust, fear, anger and frustration over student violence, not only on campus, but in communities surrounding campuses. Yet behind this immediate source of criticism lies a lack of understanding of the function of a liberal arts school and a vague suspicion that some kind of alien indoctrination goes on there. After a few years in the institution, the kids, somehow, are not the same. The change may be subtle, but it is there. There may be an undertone of resistance to the old former acquiescence to parental concepts. There may be a certain

ill-defined arrogance—especially irritating to parents who did
not go to college—but a source of some irritation even to
those who did.

So there arises an attitude that revolves around the question, "What the hell are they teaching up there?" or "Well,
they certainly have changed since I was there."

The fact is that a university is a profoundly simple institution, but its simplicity (as well as its fragility) is hidden
behind a kind of American myth. The myth is rooted in the
Jeffersonian concept of mass education—maximum years for
maximum numbers—and the relation that that concept had
to millions and millions of immigrants to whom "education"
wrought a kind of magic. Above all, it was the key to success,
but beyond that it meant status—something unattainable
under the rigid stratification of European society.

Though we are no longer a country of heavy first-genera-
tion immigrant populations, the old idea, the old sense of
"magic" hangs on. And the trouble is, there is no magic.
There is only this simple process:

For four years a university takes young men and women,
eighteen to twenty-two, lifts them out of the context of their
lives, places them in a unique setting, surrounds them with
hundreds or thousands of their own age group (but with
almost infinitely varying backgrounds) and gives them this
time to read, ask questions and receive *some* answers.

These young people are surrounded by books that they
read under vague, malleable and changing patterns termed
curricula. They are guided, occasionally prodded and sometimes plagued by a faculty, a group of specialists, a few of
whom are brilliant, most of whom are competent, a few of
whom are not.

Students at such institutions never encounter infallibility

and they rarely encounter indoctrination. They do as much teaching of each other as the faculty does of them. But a vast lot will be left unexplained, unexamined and unordered at the end of four years. No university, however structured, whatever its philosophy, can in any given span of time deliver a package of "relevant" education, neatly complete, with no loose ends dangling.

If you look at the average university catalog you would need a translator to make sense of it. The requirements seem endless, the options myriad; the offerings range from the pedestrian to the occult. The system of credits, hours, and grade point averages is more complicated than an advanced mathematical formula. But, while that might be frustrating to the entering freshman, it is not what the university is about.

This place, this unique context, this system is designed only as a beginning. It is designed to open minds a little, not to produce a final product, educated men and women. That takes the rest of their lives. It is designed to create intelligent skepticism, not to turn out cynics or doctrinaire dogmatists. Its function is to create a respect for complexities, not to render complexities simple. It is supposed to point up the worthiness of the pursuit of truth, not to serve up, neatly wrapped, the truth itself. And, the student himself is the key as to whether it succeeds or fails.

What is involved here *is* simple. It is the freedom to explore, under competent guidance or alone, to investigate, to ask, to search for facts without hindrance, to peer into all corners without let. Though it is sometimes abused and though the fact is widely misunderstood off campus, neither implicitly nor explicitly does this freedom extend to license nor divorce itself from responsibility—on the part of the faculty or the student. Freedom of this kind has classically made some

people uncomfortable and others afraid; it always will. Some
parents will always ask, Are these children up to these dis-
coveries? *Should* the lamp be cast into dark corners? Are
they ready? The answer, of course, is that they damn well
better be or we won't have much of a country left in a few
years.

The process is simple and its fragility lies in its simplicity,
not in complexity. This is because the system cannot work
when converted to the attainment of solely pragmatic ends;
it cannot work in the presence of taboos or censorship; it
withers in the face of secrecy. Universities are hard to understand precisely because they are the only institutions in the
country, the secret of whose strength lies in fragility and the
key to whose complexity is to be found in simplicity.

In the light of all this, the one thing a university cannot
become is an *instrument* for any group's pragmatic or utili-
tarian ends. Some segment of society, usually a minority, has
periodically throughout American history sought to convert
the university to an instrument serving its own purposes—
social, political, economic or religious. In recent years, faculties have risen up repeatedly to decry government contracts
for war-related research not, perforce, because they opposed
the war, but because they understood the peril of becoming
a pragmatic instrument of an arm of the government.

It is very difficult for many students and for entirely too
many faculty members to understand that the worthiness of
the cause has no bearing on the necessity for preventing the
institution itself from becoming instrumentalized in *any* cause.

A fair proportion, and perhaps the brightest proportion,
of today's dissident students, feel that a university's role must
be to convert itself into an instrument with which they can
bludgeon injustice, inequity and poverty once and for all.

They feel that the institution itself *must* become the razor's edge of social, economic and political reform. It must become institutionally involved in these issues.

Its aim *is* to equip them, as individuals, to take up what cause they will. It *is* to equip them with sharp tools to right wrongs, as individuals. But it must not itself become the *instrument*. Why?

In spite of a long and often slow and discouraging fight for what is called academic freedom, the American university over the years has largely acquired such freedom. An important part of that freedom consists of an immunity from, for instance, political retaliation; an immunity indeed, from the various groups who would *use* the university for one cause or another—and all causes are worthy to those who most ardently espouse them.

Many universities closed down in the spring of 1970 to register protest over the escalation of the war into Cambodia and to express grief over the deaths of the four Kent State students killed in a riot. Some schools half-closed and half-didn't—like my own.

Suppose universities begin closing down in the name of various causes? Suppose, for instance, as was originally planned for the fall of 1970 (the so-called "Princeton Plan"), universities shut down all over America so that the student body could actively participate in the election process? What more worthy and educational experience could there be, after all? Who could criticize the institution for thus lending itself to this worthy endeavor? Well, the answer is, just about everybody, most particularly those running for office and who hold views presumably (or at least in their own minds) anathema to the views held by student bodies and faculties. In spite of the convoluted reasoning of the American Association of

University Professors, which has encouraged this activity, this
amounts to politicalization of the university; it subjects it
therefore to retaliation. It tends to shatter its hard-won
immunity.

Certainly students have a right to campaign. They have
the right, indeed, the obligation, to work for the candidate
of their choice. They may do so just as we all do, in the
context of our prime responsibilities; by stretching the hours
of a day, by skipping classes individually. By doing what all
Americans do, that is to say, by adding political responsibilities to their other responsibilities in the priority of their lives.

We will forget Ecclesiastes only at our peril: "To everything there is a season . . . a time to plant and time to pluck
up. . . ." It is not the role of the university to *instrumentalize*
itself in any cause as an institution. If it be Cambodia now,
a political campaign in the fall, environmental activism as
an institution in the spring, when and what may it not be?
What cause is worthy of it and what cause is not?

But students are crying out for action—*now*. Is this not
a way to give it to them and hence cool the heat on campuses
next fall? Follow that reason to its labyrinth end and what
have you arrived at? Simply this: that whenever students for
whatever worthy cause cry action and now, give it to them;
turn them out of classes and endorse the action. Campuses
will be cool, all right; they will be deserted.

But the far more subtle effect will be that the university
will have destroyed its immunity from pressure groups with
countless causes. It will have undone years of the long fight
for a unique kind of freedom—a fight it won precisely because
it insisted on staying aside and standing above the strong
and emotional currents of the moment. It has stuck to that
insistence on the basis of the fact that its function was long-

range, *and for the individual* and was centered on the issues that were cumulative and from which accumulation, wisdom could be drawn by individuals as individuals.

Many students say that today's university is not relevant to their needs. When, as an institution, a university gears itself to relevance—which means, purely and simply, to that chimera which happens only at this moment to be the preoccupation of a significant proportion of people, the results can be catastrophic. A curriculum with "relevance" (in that narrow sense) as a core would be useless and outdated within the span of a very few short years. And since faculty and curricula are utterly symbiotic and inextricably intertwined, a faculty which taught only what was relevant (again in the current and narrow sense of the word) would be an anachronism within a decade.

There is another aspect to the fragility of the university which is subliminal in the minds of both faculties and laymen. One sees it, if one sees it at all, at the very edge of the periphery. It takes, roughly, twenty-two years from grammar school through the final degree to make a Ph.D. A large proportion of those who teach (those with the Ph.D.) have spent their entire lives in academia—either as students or teachers.

Graduate work, in particular, is an isolated and isolating experience. Graduate students, like somber flocks of cranes, congregate together in a community of unrelenting labor removed in all essential respects from the community around them. As professors they tend to do the same. They concern themselves with the condition of the world, of mankind and his structures (to varying degrees, depending on the discipline), but their own immersion in that condition has often been brief and superficial. This is particularly true of that new generation of scholars who were not jerked out of their pursuits by World War II or the Korean War. A couple of years as a draftee can hardly be said to count.

Now this is as it should be. The business of the academician is to be academic. A scholar is a scholar precisely because he *is* removed and precisely because he *has* spent all the major years of his life in pursuit of the specialized knowledge in his field. It has nonetheless given rise to the old saw, "If you can't do it, teach it," and to a certain constraint, say, between the businessman and the professor. Somewhere, usually, it lurks in the folds of the conflict between town and gown.

When, therefore, a faculty involves itself (either on an individual basis or on a collective one) in any cause, it should be prepared to suffer a certain alienation from "the people"— farmers, hard-hats, bankers, storekeepers, politicians, lawyers and bricklayers who, as a simple matter of the capacity to observe, usually recognize naïveté when they see it.

Beyond that, when a faculty involves itself aggressively in the affairs of the *political* community, small or large, it would be well advised to weigh its action carefully. The university's immunity, and hence the immunity of the faculty (academic freedom, if you wish) is not sacred. It hinges on a certain *quid pro quo*. That does not mean that an individual faculty member is constricted and hedged 'round with walls. It *does* mean that just as the banker or the riveter or the pilot of a plane has a bailiwick which he does not want invaded—so a faculty has a bailiwick which it can protect from invasion only so long as it respects a certain separation of empires. There are clear limits within which it can operate. There are clear limits beyond which it should not.

One of the many letters I received from university administrators came from the president of a relatively small state college in the Middle West. His institution had survived the strike in May with minimal violence. But he described the few faculty members who had helped to organize the shutdown and who had been involved in highly emotional rhetoric both off campus and on and said, ". . . we were very close to violence, but somehow these few faculty leaders did not seem to understand that. I, and the administration, of course, will be plagued by the citizens of the state for months to come by all this. Maybe these faculty members are unaware of how badly they have damaged this institution. Certainly as citizens they have the broadest kinds of rights. But do they have no attendant responsibilities?"

What is *academic freedom?* It is the freedom of a given professor in his own specialty *and only in his own specialty* to teach as he sees fit in his own classroom. It is the freedom to do research without hindrance or let in his own specialty. But the American Association of University Professors who, in effect, took from 1915 to 1940 to work out the definition of academic freedom, made explicit these "duties correlative with rights." The teacher "should be careful not to introduce into his teaching controversial matter *which has no relation to his subject* [italics mine]." The AAUP went on to describe obligations as well as rights and stated, "but his special position in the community imposes special obligations. As a man of learning and an education officer, he should remember that the public may judge his profession and his institution by his utterances. Hence he should at all times be accurate, should exercise proper restraint, should show respect for the opinions of others, and should make every effort to indicate that he is not an institutional spokesman."

During the "strike" of May, 1970, how many faculty members at how many universities honored *their own explicit code of conduct* and refrained from *ad hoc* classroom discussions

on Cambodia, Nixon, or any number of other issues completely removed from their expertise? During those highly
emotional days, how many faculty members were "at all times
accurate" in their statements about Cambodia, Nixon, the
military-industrial complex, and other current topics? How
many of them at the thousands of rallies and gatherings "ex-
ercised appropriate restraint" as "men of learning"? How
many of the fiery faculty speakers "showed respect for the
opinions of others"?

The questions are rhetorical. I can only remark that if (in
their own defense)—at the drop of a soft felt hat—faculties
feel free to challenge even an implicit violation of their own
academic freedom by appealing to the AAUP (which they
most assuredly do), are they all as quick to abide by the
obligations that are tied to the rights? My own answer is
that a significant number are not. It is a one-sided coin far
too often. The "rights" are affirmed over and over again. The
"obligations" are simply not observed.

Does this apply to a majority of faculty members across
the land? Certainly not, but the minority, however small, perform a disservice to the majority and to the institutions in
which they teach, all out of proportion to their numbers. By
word and action they misrepresent to the public, to boards
of regents, to legislators and to alumni both the institution
and the faculty as a whole. They leave the beleaguered president with battles to fight which he can rarely win. Above
all, they threaten academic freedom itself because they misrepresent it.

A university cannot exist without academic freedom. It
lies at the very heart of its function. In the days and years
to come, the public, boards, and all of the university's critics
must be informed that the vast majority of faculty members

abide by all the terms encompassed in the phrase, not by just those rules that suit them.

So that is a generalized picture of a basically simple and fragile institution—an institution of enormous importance to America. It is now beleaguered—not merely by the firebrands, the violent tacticians dedicated to its destruction, but by many other forces.

What, one may ask, of the people most concerned? What of the nonmilitant students—what of the vast majority who abhor violence and want an education? What, in other words, of the younger generation? Well, the whole matter, in the end, turns on what they do and what commitments they make. And so it revolves, too, around how accurate they are in their appraisal of themselves and of my generation. Let us consider, then, in what ways we agree and in what ways we disagree. Let us ascertain the view from where *I* sit, however remote it seems at the moment to the twenty-year-old who looks upon life from the green, sharp wonder of his years.

Chapter 3

The Uncommitted Young

BEING young (and it seems absurd that it needs assertion, but it does: everyone was once young) is an intense and deeply introspective condition. Nature provided the young with certain endowments calculated to protect them from their own foolishness. They are strong—and thus can extricate themselves from positions in which they never should have gotten in the first place. In lieu of judgment, which is the product of age and experience, they are given quick reflexes, insouciance and abundant energy. Experience and judgment are nearly inseparable entities, the latter growing out of the former. This may not be an invariable relationship, but it nearly always is.

This fact assumes considerable importance in the light of America's weird current preoccupation with its youth. I do not presume to know from whence this preoccupation came. Americans consider America to be a "youthful" country—which, in fact, it is not. It has been a democratic republic for nearly two centuries and in the light of the dozens of new countries born in the last thirty years, we are at least middle-aged. My own generation go to absurd lengths to "be youthful"—including the "pal" relationship with their children by virtue of which they even adopt the argot of their progeny. All the media emphasize youthfulness and the marketplaces are glutted with creams, oils, salves, wigs and ointments guaranteed to restore skin, hair and teeth to their youthful condition. Perhaps the attempt to restore some lost magic (foolish as it is, since all life is magic) is a harmless, if embarrassing, phenomenon. But the repetitious and seriously uttered cry, "We must listen to our youth!" is not harmless.

On campus and off, the adjuration, "We must listen to our youth," has been relentlessly repeated over and over again. And listen to them we do. I doubt that there is a major magazine in America that has not in the past year or two given over a whole issue to the problems, prattlings, philosophies, sophistries, peculiarities, longings and expectations of youth. Nor is it merely a matter of "special issues"; *each* issue of most major American magazines carries a weekly or monthly overburden of information on what youth are doing, saying, thinking or demanding.

Television has given over special after special to youth as if, indeed, there were no Americans but youthful Americans; as if, indeed, only *they* have a corner on anguish; only *they* feel deeply about the problems of our age; only *they* have solutions. It is in this latter respect that I and my kind grow most indignant. The one thing they are the least adept at is propounding workable solutions for the problems that confront *all* of us. They are the least adept because they are the least experienced. They are the least adept because their judgment is the least developed by time and circumstance.

The utter monotony of the cry, "We must listen to our

youth," almost always carries with it an unspoken but strongly implied corollary, "because only they can save us." I, for one (and I somehow get the feeling that I have a lot of non-youth company) would rather go down with the old ship as she is than to step into the lifeboat which youth is presently lowering (ineptly) from the davits. I see no evidence that that thing will float as long as the wreckage of America (a wreckage they, not I, presume to be the condition of the vessel).

In other societies throughout time, age and experience have been, in varying degrees, the prerequisites for leadership. Even the most primitive societies were governed by a council of elders. The most advanced and successful societies had more elaborate and intricate senior structures, but they were senior. Youth was indeed listened to, at the proper time in its development and to the precise degree that it had something to say. Young Turks did sometimes overturn the structure—if their plans were sound enough and their appeal rational enough.

But a very large number of extremely loquacious American youths, whose plans, if they can be called plans at all, are shot through with inanities, are now attended to by the older generation as if they were sages—as if they had some secret, exclusively their own—which will solve all our problems—*if only we will listen.* Well, we have listened, ad infinitum. And the result for me and many of my kind is a rather simple conclusion. I think we had better keep our own hands on the wheel until youthful zealots give us a little more evidence that they know how to steer.

Another result of the total media's (television, radio, newspapers, magazines and books) deep and ponderous preoccupation with youth is that youth itself garners its image of itself from us, the older generation. There is a certain irony in that. Youth tends to believe what it hears and sees of itself. The irony lies in the fact that the picture my generation draws of the younger generation is a badly flawed picture—and so youth's picture of itself is flawed. If it is to govern, as govern it will in due course—one way or another, I would ardently hope that it first finds itself—at least to the extent of seeing itself in its own mirror and not in ours.

For example, on May 11, 1970, *Time* magazine carried an essay (in a blue box at that) by a young lady, Linda Eldredge, nineteen. It was a sad and personal little thing accompanied by Miss Eldredge's sad, wan and weary photograph. Linda felt "overwhelmingly helpless." She and her friends felt "horror and grief and rage." The essay goes on in the same jejune way as a hundred others I have read. Linda had worked for Humphrey and he lost. Her reaction? ". . . we worked our hearts out for him and had them broken. And hardened. [At nineteen!!] At Chicago we grew up and felt our youth withering. [At nineteen!!] . . . The cities are still dying; much of the countryside is dead. [Have you seen the countryside, Linda, with your eyes open?] . . . What are we supposed to do with our lives? [How about trying to live them.] How do we go about solving the complex problems of our world? [You won't solve them. Nobody ever has.] . . . Our parents hate us, our politicians desert us. [You mean like the Kennedys? Like Medgar Evers?] Our hopes simply grew old and died. [At nineteen!] I sound as if I am wallowing in self-pity because the world is too harsh. I'm not. I am only very tired." [At nineteen!]

My first reaction to Miss Eldredge's little essay, filled as it was with misinterpretations, but above all filled with wan world-weariness, was to send her a bottle of Geritol. My second reaction was to write *Time* magazine asking it to cease and desist running material seriously which belongs in the junior high school literary quarterly. But Miss Eldredge, of course, hardened heart and all, is reflecting the picture of herself and the world which *we* have drawn for her. One day, hopefully, she will see herself as she is and ought to be—without the need for Geritol.

The misconceptions, erroneous conclusions, mistinterpretations and canards in so much youthful writing, in so many "rap" sessions, in so many interviews, fall into monotonous categories. That does not matter, except that we read it (my generation) and listen to it and take it seriously. Not only that, we mistake adolescent glibness for profundity and if we continue to stay off-center in this fashion we are likely to end up with American foreign policy determined by majority vote in the eighth grade. It is a vicious and serious indictment of my own generation that we cannot seem to act our ages and accept our responsibilities. Why? Is it because the world is too much for us? If so, it is certainly too much for our children—and we can hardly blame them for a full measure of despair.

I doubt that adolescent sensitivities, moods, feelings of loneliness and apartness have changed much from generation to generation. I doubt that the process of growing up, accompanied as it is by heightened feelings in all respects and above all by feelings of enormous expectations, has altered very much in a thousand years. It is an age characterized by a desire to do everything, feel everything, try everything and be everything. In spite of complex inner turmoil, it is an age of utter simplicity in that the perfectibility of man and his institutions is thoroughly feasible. The only things that prevent the immediate attainment of Nirvana are man-made structures and habits which, after all, need only to be torn down or altered in some simple way, to obtain justice, equity, love and joy for all people for all time.

What we, my generation, have abysmally failed to teach the younger generation is that it doesn't work that way. We have failed to teach them that the structures that stand athwart man's perfectibility are not really governments, not bureaucracies, not politicians, not mores, not habits. *Man* is the problem. Miss Eldredge's real problem is not Chicago, not dying cities, not war, not President Johnson. Miss Eldredge's problem is Miss Eldredge. And the larger problem is that inside himself man is not only good but he is also evil. The fight inside man between his own good and his own evil is as old as man. It is a battle which has intrigued philosophers from Zeno to Sartre. Miss Eldridge asks the question, What are we supposed to do with our lives? And the only really honest reply is, <u>Live so as to understand the battle within yourself and so as to give the odds to the good in you.</u> Will that answer satisfy Miss Eldredge? Of course not. Will it satisfy the majority of this particular generation? Of course not. Yet ultimately, if they are to function maturely (and at this juncture in history they must) that is the one thing they must understand about themselves above all others.

In the meantime let us consider what a great many of the younger generation *think* their problems are. These categories are drawn not only from the thousands of letters I have received, but from the essays, talks, rap sessions and conversations which the young initiate and conduct. I am not here concerned with the militant, with the righteous firebrand, but with those who are standing by, uncommitted, critical, vaguely rebellious and inherently confused.

It is widely believed that this younger generation is unique in that it has "grown up" with the Damocletian sword in the form of the H-bomb hanging over its head. The assertion is constantly made that this is the first of any generation to live in a milieu of imminent collective catastrophe and that that circumstance has conditioned it and made its values basically different from any preceding generation—including my own.

This argument overlooks some very fundamental facts. I was in my twenties when the bomb was invented. If it has conditioned them, it has likewise conditioned me and my generation. I submit that it has not. It has altered our view of the role that diplomacy must play. It has changed the world power structure. It has not been a basic conditioner of what man thinks of man.

The younger generation in America, H-bomb notwithstanding, grew up more secure (in the proper sense of that word) than any generation in the history of America—and probably it grew up more secure than any generation in the world in modern times, that is, since 1500.

When you caught pneumonia in 1930, you almost always died; the same for scarlet fever, blood poisoning, streptococci infection, spinal meningitis, typhus, typhoid and innumerable *common* diseases of which most of the younger generation have never heard.

The average life span of the American male in 1900 was in the early forties. In those days there were no obstetricians. Surgeons used meat axes more often than scalpels and if the patient avoided postoperative shock, he usually died of resultant infections—no penicillin, no antibiotics, no blood plasma no vitamins. As a consequence superficial battle wounds were more often than not fatal. The child mortality rate as of 1900 would curdle the blood of today's twenty-year-old girl.

As for mass catastrophe, man has always lived just beneath its shadow. The Black Death killed a million Britons, a third of the country's population, in one swift visitation in the fourteenth century. Ten thousand people a day were dying of it in Byzantium. Plague and famine besieged millions upon millions of Indians, Chinese and Russians. They died in such massive numbers that whole cities and provinces had to be left to the dead.

It is true that mankind can now destroy itself via the pushing of a button. But if you insist that this makes you and me different in our basic approach to the business of living and dying, you overlook not only the fact that mankind has always lived under the sword of Damocles, you overlook another commonality we share. Collective death is no more awesome to the dying than individual death. No one gets out of this life alive—even your generation. Death is awesome, no less nor more so, because it comes to you or me when we are alone or in the company of millions. So no Damocletian sword accounts either for your ethic or for mine. The only fact that matters is that we are tenuously mortal. And that mortality we share—you and I and everyone who lives or has ever lived—or ever will.

Nothing is more constantly set forth by these spokesmen for the younger generation than the pernicious effect of my generation's "materialism." Materialism is so much a part of the rhetoric of the young that in the drumbeat of the use of the word, in the iteration, reiteration and repetition of the phrase it has lost all meaning. It conjures up vague visions of blindly greedy people pursuing "things" in some mad rat race.

My nephew, in a rebuttal to the initial piece I wrote about his generation, referred with disgust to "the psychically unsat-

isfying pursuit of material comfort" which had so characterized my generation and had, by implication, thus visited upon
his generation the miseries of crassness and blindness.

When I read my nephew's letter (a long and courteous
one, by the way) a series of pictures flashed across my mind.
The first picture was of his father (my brother), the somewhat
aquiline face deeply lined, the tall body beginning to stoop
(he is fifty-four), the look of vague exhaustion. The second
picture that flashed into my mind was of my nephew himself,
behind the wheel of his father's speedboat—a picture of joyous freedom—materialistic as hell. He was home, that summer, from Lawrence University, all tuition and expenses paid
there—paid by his father's "psychically unsatisfying pursuit
of material comfort."

If there was anything in my brother's life he never sought,
it was material comfort. And thinking about him, it occurred
to me that almost more than anyone else I knew he represented my generation, what it was after and why it was after
what it was after. And I thought, My God, how can a bright
young man, my nephew, have eyes and not see, ears and
not hear and a mind and not use it?

My nephew, as it happens, represents, I think, his generation (that waiting, uncommitted portion of it) almost as much
as his father represents his. So from these two people's lives
let me attack the wearisome charge that "materialism" is the
greasy heritage left the son by the father. I need no biographi-
cal sketches, no character analyses: these are two thoroughly
decent people, father and son—both of whom love each other
and the country.

After that long-forgotten, faraway war, World War II, my
brother had a wife, a few dollars saved, and he had to do
something; he had to make a living. (As an aside, let me

say that this point will come in the lives of almost all of the new "non-materialistic" generation and I must admit that I await its arrival with some glee because I want to see how many of them think it will go away if they don't look it in the face. Affluent America may be, but not affluent enough to sustain a whole generation of indigents.)

In any event, my brother rented a tiny office in an old building. There was room for a secondhand desk, a filing cabinet, a used typewriter, and a typing table for his wife, who acted as secretary. Horatio Alger is *not* coming up, but a point of sorts is. Then he had some cards printed that said "Toole Insurance Agency," and then he started walking up and down the street on the soles of his shoes, dropping in on businesses saying, "My name is Toole. Here is my card. If you ever need any insurance, I hope you will call on me."

Then he went around to a few young fellows, with maybe a backhoe and a few tools, who were trying to build houses and he said, "Why don't you bid on some city, or county, or state buildings—and I will talk some insurance company into writing your bond." I went with him once and the young "contractor," to whom he suggested that he bid on a piece of county road, scratched his head, looked around at his equipment (one old truck, a rusting bulldozer, vintage 1938, and a few odds and ends of blades and parts) and said, "Jesus, with this equipment?" But the deal was made, the bid was won and the bond was written. And in between my brother walked up and down the street on the soles of his shoes and tried to sell insurance. His wife kept policy numbers and renewal dates in a plastic-covered book with green tabs. And for a long time there were very few tabs.

Now it is true that my brother wanted a house, a car, a refrigerator and some things. Cavemen also wanted caves.

But is that why he was walking up and down the street on
the soles of his shoes? No. Was it that he loved insurance?
No, the business is dull. He was doing it because he had
to make a living, indeed. But the real reason is what my
nephew doesn't understand. The real reason is what millions
of young Americans don't understand.

Men have always engaged with other men, largely to understand themselves. They compete and gamble to see where
they can go. They have to test themselves to see where they
can go, to find things out about themselves. When they seem
thus mostly to be looking outward, they are mostly looking
inward.

But it is a great puzzlement to me that his son should
regard this process as the "psychically unsatisfying pursuit
of material comfort," and that he should think that all his
father was after was a house, a refrigerator and two cars.

There is really no way for men to avoid taking the measure
of themselves. By gambling, by risking, by working and thinking. What they really want to know is this: How far along
the dream of what I could be can I really go? What can I
build from nothing? How good am I? How will I act if I
fail? All on my own, out of what I am, can I make something
work? Who, after all, am I? The only way to find out is
to do these things and push myself. The only way to find
out is to engage life on some level, any level, head-on.

It is true that the by-product of my brother's endeavor
was a nice house on a hill, two cars, and a cabin on a lake.
My generation was very successful, so there is affluence. What
the younger generation fails so abysmally to understand is
that the "things" were by-products. Beyond sufficiency they
never mattered at all. Very, very few Americans sought things

as things. It's the younger generation, via their acute consciousness of the things, who are the materialists.

Closely allied to this charge of materialism is the accusation
that my generation has created, in the form of cybernated
technology, a voracious monster which is, among other things,
rapaciously destroying all that is good and beautiful in the
country. It is certainly true that there has been a technological
explosion of great magnitude since World War II and that
my generation has presided over the most explosive portion
of its growth. It is also true that this explosion has created
grave problems—not the least of which is a great acceleration
in the process of pollution and environmental degradation.

But, again, there is this strange, shallow blindness in the
view so many of the younger generation take of technology.
It is true that if they do not control it (in their time) it will
eat them up. And they will not control it if they do not understand it. They will not control it if their only knowledge of
it is, as my nephew expressed it, that it is destroying the spirit
of man and the quality of life—"this headlong rush toward
greater affluence through technology."

Let us first consider environmental degradation. The
process is a very old one. In a sense, when the first man
put the first plow into the first piece of earth, this degradation
began. The swift industrialization of America after the Civil
War led to a rapid increase in the pollution of rivers and
lakes and in the destruction of forests. The country was huge
and its resources were so apparently unlimited that no one
paid much heed to reclamation or to worrying about a finite
ecosystem.

After World War II another technological burst occurred
and the pace of degradation increased. In the early 1950's

(before most of the present younger generation was born) scientists began seriously to study the effects of the emissions from industrial plants, the effects of the new chemical fertilizers on rivers and streams, the danger to animal and plant life from insecticides and other technological developments.

By the early 1960's conservation groups across the country were springing up like mushrooms and were concertedly attacking pollution and environmental degradation of all kinds. By the middle 60's, the courts were crammed by actions in equity, by injunctions and other legal processes aimed at punitive or preventive action. By the late 60's the media had taken up the cry and added immeasurably to the pressure being exerted on polluting industries. County after county and then state after state and, finally, the Federal Government began to set standards for all manner of technological processes which contributed to pollution of air or water. These standards, and tough ones, are now in effect in many states and this is only the beginning.

It is simply absurd for the younger generation to say (1) that my generation caused pollution and is leaving them a wasteland "because of our headlong rush toward affluence through technology" and (2) that we are doing nothing about it. The simple fact is that we are the only generation that ever *has* done anything about it. A national conservation and anti-pollution campaign of unprecedented magnitude was mounted and is being carried forth by my generation and there is not the remotest possibility that we will weaken in this endeavor. The younger generation which only very recently has joined this fight, would do well to tone down its rhetoric and join the rest of us in the courts, at hearings and in the legislative and congressional corridors where the action is.

Of greater consequence, however, is the vague, emotion-ridden, ill-informed attack by the young on "technology." There is a kind of childish atavism involved in this in which at least part of the solution is to flee from this rampant monster into the fastnesses of some pristine wilderness (a commune, perhaps).

The fact is that technology is precisely what man makes of it and does with it; the fact is that computers *don't* think, men do. The fact is that the plowshare and the sword are both made by technology from the same metal. And the further fact is this: that a technological society which can land men on the moon three feet from target site over a distance of 250,000 miles can most assuredly turn it upon itself, given the will and the necessity, and solve problems of pollution. What a dim and foggy vision it is that sees so little of the marvelous things that technology can do to make man's life better and more joyous—and sees only the problems it creates. How essentially absurd it is to be so young and yet so fearful. The fact is that problems have always spun off from each new step man has taken; the fact is that whenever he has ventured into new realms to reveal new wonders, the step itself creates new problems—which must then be faced and solved.

If what the younger generation wants is the total solution now to each new problem man creates by facing into the unknown, and trying the untried, then it should recognize that what it fears and what it does not understand is not man's works but man himself. Because since man first dropped out of the trees and became man, he has been driven by a thing deep within his spirit which says, "Risk it—and move on." If you, the younger generation, decide not to risk it and not to move on, if you decide that faith in your own capabil-

ities is insufficient to sustain you, and, to some degree, to
bend time and life to your will, at least grant us that that
was your choice—and not an inheritance from us.

Another category which seems so to preoccupy the young
is that we (my generation) were conditioned and frozen into
a rigid mold either by the Depression (about which ap-
pallingly few of them know anything at all) or (and the con-
tradiction does not seem to trouble them at all) we were
conditioned by growing up in some sublimely rural, pastoral,
untroubled age. As my nephew put it, "We face floods of
problems . . . my uncle never had to think about . . . the
bomb, cybernetics, etc."

Many of us *were* indeed "conditioned" by the Depression.
It was a lean, hard time for millions of Americans. And,
as the recent book *Hard Times* (edited by Studs Terkel)
makes clear, it resulted in a kind of closeness, an *élan*, a
new feeling of wholeness. It left little bitterness, less rigidity
and no livid scars which we bequeath as a legacy to the young.

As for the sublimely pastoral, untroubled age and the
"floods of problems" we did *not* have to face, let me briefly
refer to my brother again. When he was his son's age (maybe
a little older), he found himself lying with half his face in
a mud puddle. He was aware that there was a skim of ice
on the water. And he couldn't make himself move. What
he really wanted to do was die—he wanted to die right there
in the pastoral surroundings of a little town called Benweir.
But circumstances wouldn't oblige him. He had troops to lead,
but he just lay there—full of exhaustion and terror. He
thought, "They will court-martial me and imprison me for
the rest of my life. But that is infinitely better than moving."
And he lay there in the freezing mud puddle for a long time
and quit. His soul froze up and his spirit had withered a

long time ago anyway. Then after a little while he got up
and went off and did what he had to do. He reached down
inside himself, into some deep reservoir of reserve and
courage, stood up very straight and led his troops into a battle
he was utterly convinced that he could not survive. Though
he was grievously wounded, the enemy never obliged him
by killing him—even in a quiet pasture. He got a Silver Star
for that, but that did not matter. All that mattered was that
the courage was there.

If you go back before the war, there was enough anguish,
from inside my brother's self, from trying to find himself and
prove himself, to fill my nephew's reservoir of despair for
a long time to come.

I was my nephew's age once, though he cannot, I am
sure, envision it. My experiences were different from my
brother's—although one of my clearer memories was how
I was going to get from the stern to the bow of a ship because
the deck was so slippery with blood, human entrails and raw
pieces of bodies.

Five years earlier, when I was eighteen—it was a lousy,
rotten, cruel, gluttonous world. I had, it is true, the choice
of removing myself from it, but I didn't. I didn't sink into
a sea of despondency either. But I often felt despair, deep
frustration, and a kind of abiding sense of loss. I felt rudder-
less and alone. But, says my nephew; but, says most of his
generation, "We have floods of problems you never had to
think about."

It is simply a hard and uncompromising fact that they do
not. Worse, they do not even understand their problems. They
face the same problems everyone always has. They think they
arise from the bomb, from an immoral war in the Far East,
from pollution, from materialism, from technology. But these

things are external. They are not even unique. They are merely another face of the same one-million-faceted face that has always been staring at one utterly naked man. *He*'s your problem. You.

A proportion of any generation has sought escape. HEW estimates that there are roughly 6,000,000 alcoholics in my generation. We have entirely too many wreckages of human beings on a hundred skid rows. They are our dropouts—and they represent part of our failure.

But you, the younger generation, so quick to seize on our failures, so righteously pointing the finger of blame, so pontifically clicking off our shortcomings, what of your failures *already?* How many of you have copped out even before you tried anything to fail at? How many of you have fallen down before the wind even blew? How many people do you have *already* in dropout cells all over America?

The commune. They *say* they simply won't live by our values; they won't play our game. That's what they say. But when you talk to them, the rationalization in it jumps out like a weird jack-in-the-box. Because it is not from us or our values of our society that they are fleeing. It is not from materialism or technology or the establishment that they are running. They are running from themselves. Alas, they take into the commune with them every nightmare they fled—plus one, the fact of their fleeing. And still, they will have to walk up and down paths of the commune on the soles of their sandals, and, in the end, face the same thing every man has had to face. And the beads won't help and the pot won't help, and the needle won't help and the gurus won't help—nor even the hair and the beards. They are to hide behind. But where, really, is the hole in which you can hide from yourself? Is that what the guru seeks in his navel?

They seek a new "life style" (another one of those drumbeat words in the rhetoric from the steps of the administration building). It is never quite clear what they mean, but it doesn't matter if it is repeated often and vehemently enough. There is nothing wrong with a new "life style" if they are tired of the old or find it wanting. Indeed, I hope they find it. But if they mean by new "life style" what I *think* they mean, sorrowfully, they will never find it. It is wrapped up in several of those old (and, hence, probably unworthy) verities: you cannot dance without paying the piper, you cannot have a right unless an obligation is stuck to it, and you cannot be free until you are sure that your freedom costs no one else his.

There is another consideration and it has to do with power. It is a consideration which the younger campus generation might bear in mind.

Commencement addresses are, at best, bad. It is customary somewhere along the string of clichés which constitute such addresses for the speaker to say, "And so we, the older generation, pass on to you, the younger, the torch of liberty with all the profound responsibilities inherent in holding that torch high. . . ." This conjures up in one's mind not only a horde of seniors emerging from the auditorium doors with torches, but also (once the torches are stored) slipping easily behind the executive desk to run the company. It doesn't work that way.

The company—and the country—are actually being run by some very tough and experienced people (thirty to seventy) who not only don't give a damn about torches, but who have no intention of giving up hard-won power to anyone.

In terms of judgment, know-how, toughness and cleverness

they are in their prime. There might be some doubt that they could beat the senior at the one-hundred-yard dash, but there is very little doubt that they could beat him at most other things—particularly their own game.

So the senior's task is not simply to take over the relinquished reins, it is to become good enough and strong enough and clever enough to grab for them. He is likely to find that that is not only a very difficult task, but a long one. The forty-year-old vice president of a medium-sized company has at least twenty more tough years in him; so does the foreman, so does the editor, so does the insurance agent, so does the accountant, the lawyer.

In almost all endeavors the theory is one thing, the practice another. And it is more than a waiting game; it is a working game. In almost all endeavors *ideas* matter greatly. But what matters most about them is: Do they work?

This, I have found, usually puzzles a good many emergent graduates. They have grown accustomed in academia to placing considerable value on ideas in the abstract. This is proper and they should—because it is probably the only period in their lives (unless they become professors) when the abstract will weigh heavier than the pragmatic. Sometimes it takes a while to find that out.

Whatever "life style" the young want, and however they want to change the rules and values; however they wish to place spirit above bread (and in all these desires and ambitions I laud them and wish them luck), they should at least be prepared for the ubiquitous man peering into their eyes with the incessant question, "Yes, but does it work?"

Oddly enough, revolution and different economic approaches don't change that. The Communist motto, "To each according to needs, from each according to his ability," some-

how got turned around into "Have you met your quota?"
or "Yes, but does it work?" Socialist economic systems, as
a matter of fact, are even more conscious of utility than are
capitalist.

Millions, perhaps billions, of human beings are living bar-
ren and joyless lives. Hundreds of thousands of Americans
are living bleakly not only below poverty levels, but below
the level of human decency in any regard. Countless human
beings, untroubled by poverty, live narrowly, a canyon-width
away from the potential in them for love and happiness.

All that, we are agreed, must change. Only ideas will
change it. No matter what we do or how we do it, the man
will always be there asking, "Yes, but does it work?"

Chapter 4

The Violent Ones

How great a proportion of the student population in America is violent; that is, how many readily and by prearranged plan seek to turn a rally or a peaceful protest into violent channels? No one knows, because the proportion varies from campus to campus and from time to time. There is, however, general agreement on the part of those who have studied student dissent in general, that the proportion is very small.

How great a proportion of the student population, not philosophically oriented toward violence, has turned, nonetheless, to violence in mob form once a confrontation took place? Again, no one knows, but the number is significantly larger. Still, in relation to the 7,000,000 students on American campuses, it is a minuscule percentage.

Yet once again, the numbers game (even if this matter could be quantified) would be meaningless, because over and above proportions and percentages, like an ugly umbrella, there hangs one incontrovertible fact: Campus after campus in America has been ripped and torn to pieces; the fabric of dialogue, decency, civility and order has been rent to shreds; the structure of learning, teaching and scholarship has repeatedly been twisted into grotesque caricatures of what a university should be; up has become down, wrong has become right and white has become black.

The contagion, the attitude, the atmosphere has spread across the land so that even in the many universities where violence has not occurred (a great majority), fear and tension have distorted the function and inhibited the operation of a thousand institutions. To "keep the peace" faculties and administrations have subserviently (usually for the worse) changed the *modus operandi;* they have pandered to absurd student proposals; they have admitted guilt where none existed. Entirely too many faculty members, for reasons complex but probably rooted in equal parts of fear and a desire for popularity, have joined students in causes which are not causes and in functions which have neither teaching nor learning potential.

On the basis of an oft-expressed axiom which will bear up under no rational scrutiny at all, namely, "Any experience at all is an educational experience," faculty members have participated, for instance, in inane "educational" experiments. Two recent reports by Lewis B. Mayhew (1969) and the Hazen Foundation (1968) endorse student "ideas" and call for these reforms in higher education: abolition of course requirements, departments, attendance rules (few universities have them anyway), grades, lectures, *teacher-dominated discussions* [italics mine] and the notion of objectivity as an educational tool.[1]

That kind of nonsense is taken seriously, indeed with pon-

---

[1] "What Happened to the Free University?" *Saturday Review,* June 20, 1970.

derous sobriety, by entirely too many students and faculty members. A teacher who in his own field, broad or narrow, isn't infinitely better informed than his students should, under no circumstances, be teaching at all. To eschew "objectivity as an educational tool" at the same time that you eliminate the teacher is a genuine exercise in anti-intellectualism—as well as in absurdity.

But these ideas, these adoptions, these endorsements, these inanities are the spin-off products of violence. So what can be said about campus violence? Such violence has been studied repeatedly on a "case study" basis. Specific riots have been chronicled with all the intensity of a Capote performance—who did what, precisely where and to whom? What was the Dean of Students thinking as he was hustled from his office? What was Howard Johnson thinking as he threw the lighted flare into the administration building? What were the precise roles of the SDS, the Third World Liberation Front, the Black Student Union? What were the rankling issues and why and for how long had they been simmering?

The trouble with such case studies (and in conglomerate form they *do* have merit)[2] is that in the end they do not answer basic questions, they tend to be parochial chronicles. Lessons in generalized form are almost impossible to draw from them. Nonetheless, let me begin a generalized discussion of student violence with at least the skeleton of a case study: Kent State, Ohio. The reason is obvious: Four students were killed there.

Kent State was in no sense a militant school. Its student

---

[2] For several of the best, see Julian Foster and Durward Long, eds., "Seven Case Studies," Section III in *Protest*, William Morrow and Company, Inc., 1970, pp. 225–345.

body was largely drawn from middle America, a region hardly known for radicalism. There had been few harbingers of trouble.

It started not on campus but in the town of Kent itself, a paradigm of near-somnolent rectitude and conformity. It started on a humid Friday night in the spring when, as in most college towns, especially with finals approaching, the beer stubes and taverns fill up with students. The mood was light—all was well.

And then it turned ugly and it turned ugly quickly. Students began pouring out onto the street—a goodly number of them carrying a considerable ballast of beer or liquor. Several students began throwing bottles; a half dozen climbed on the roof of a car and, jumping in unison, crushed in its top. Then, up and down the street it spread; the window smashing began, fires were set in ashcans. In a matter almost of minutes the town of Kent had a full-fledged riot on its hands. Kent's citizens were terror-stricken. Property damage was extensive and wanton.

Why did this first event in a series of tragic events occur? Is it too much to ask that question of the students who wrought the damage? They and they alone can answer. And they have not answered. Had the community of Kent visited some awful affront on them? Had the town of Kent maligned them, abused them? Had it damaged them? Was this, then, a matter of revenge? Ask the violent students. They and they alone can answer those questions. If Kent, as a community, had somehow damaged the students it must have been a very severe damage indeed to justify such retribution.

But that was only the beginning. Finally, that Friday night, the police emptied the bars and, firing tear gas, pushed the students back to the campus. And the police? It would take

no Capote, no long interviews to surmise that, grossly outnumbered and with fierce violence swirling around them, they
were afraid. And they had every right to be.

Incredibly, in view of Friday night's rampage, in view of
wholesale outlawry and the terrorization of an entire community, Kent State's administration granted the students permission to hold a rally on campus the next night.

In view of a now palpably ugly mood, why did the administration grant that permission? The Kent State incident will
be investigated and reinvestigated, but either one of two things
were true irrespective of the inevitable administration's defense of itself: Either it was afraid *not* to grant the permit
(in which event it was culpable because *somewhere* along
the line an administration must take a stand on student
discipline—and if the sacking of Kent was not that place,
where is it?) or the administration simply did not understand
the nature of violence. It was, in any event, an incredibly
bad decision. It gave the militant violent students a weekend
in which to plan. It implicitly gave the student body the im-
pression that it had "control."

It began again. A campus dance was violently disrupted.
Militants attacked the ROTC building (a symbol, however
absurd, of military evil on almost every American campus).
When firemen arrived, the students fought them and cut the
fire hoses.

Kent's mayor, who did not consult the university administration, called the governor for help from the National
Guard. The governor sent the Guard, again without checking
with the university administrators. Were the mayor and the
governor wrong in failing to keep in touch with the President
of Kent? Probably. But the mayor, particularly with Friday
night's rampage on his mind—and with the campus itself now

burning—may have had abundant evidence that Kent State had irretrievably lost control of Kent State.

Enter now the National Guard, weary and bleary-eyed from three nights running in a tense situation regarding a teamsters' strike elsewhere. Enter now the National Guard, ill-trained in riot control—and, if typical of the majority of Guard units elsewhere—ill-trained for much of anything.

It is no secret (and particularly no secret from students) that the National Guard in America (generally) has been a political boondoggle of long standing and that Congress has tried for years either to abolish it or at least to bring its training up to minimal military standards—and has failed.

Enter now the *Ohio* National Guard, one of the few Guard forces in the country permitted to carry live ammunition in their M1's. And enter now the National Guard (500 of them) confronted with this scene: campus trees burning from gasoline tossed on them by rioting students, groups of students running from building to building throwing rocks and breaking windows—and students armed with rocks and clubs, closing in on a confused, weary, leaderless (or almost so) and terribly frightened and ill-prepared Guard unit. And so there were shots fired—and so in a moment or two, four Kent State students lay dead—not one of them an activist, not one of them violent.

In the investigation that will follow, blame will be weighed out carefully and apportioned here and there. A minute-by-minute chronicling of events will be meticulously set forth. There will, undoubtedly, be an introduction setting forth student grievances, general and particular, and that will be that. But in fact that will not be that. There are some things that need to be said about Kent State because they bear on every institution of higher learning in America—and because they bear on America itself. The Scranton Report just published is detailed, graphic and illuminating, but there is little new in it.

For instance, Allison Krause was one of the students killed at Kent State. She was pretty, nonviolent, quiet. In an anguished statement after her death, her father said, "Is dissent a crime? Is this a reason for killing her? Have we come to such a state in this country that a young girl has to be shot because she disagrees with her government?"

With all deference to Mr. Krause, and with due regard for his anguish and grief, he should, and in a sense he must, know why his daughter died. She was not killed because she disagreed with her government. Most of us do some of the time. She died because violence, once let loose, makes no distinction between the innocent and the guilty, the young or the old, the male or the female.

One of the National Guardsmen's wives remarked the following day, "My husband is no murderer. He was afraid. He was sure that they were going to be overrun by those kids." And the fact is, he is *not* a murderer.

The immediate cause of the death of Allison Krause was a bullet fired by a National Guardsman. But the real cause lies elsewhere; the real blame *is* assignable, the Scranton Report and the report of the grand jury notwithstanding. Allison Krause—and her three equally innocent fellow students—were killed by every student who threw a rock, wielded a club, tossed gasoline on a fire, cut a fire hose or broke a window. Allison Krause was killed because militant students let loose the dogs of riot. She was killed precisely by those who incited to riot and by those who participated in it.

All over America students at universities and colleges reacted to the events at Kent State (tying their strikes and demonstrations into the Cambodian situation, ROTC and a dozen other causes) with fierce rhetoric condemning Nixon, war, pollution, the military-industrial complex, the establishment, and in one form or another they memorialized the four dead students. Not once in those miasmic days in early May did I hear or read at my university any condemnation of the students at Kent who involved themselves in riot. Not once was mention made of those who lit the fuse on the bomb which exploded at Kent State.

On my own campus, with thousands of students sitting on the oval before the administration building, listening to harangue after speech after harangue, not once did I hear one critical word of the students who set off, guided and engaged in the violence at Kent. Those who spoke included two ministers and a priest. They had harshly critical things to say about America and most of its institutions. And they spoke of peace. But not once did they point the finger of guilt at those who broke the peace. Men of God and men of peace, faculty affiliates all, and not once did they call the guilty guilty.

Perhaps that is because men of God and men of peace know so little of violence, but for the life of me I cannot understand why anyone who has lived beyond puberty, read more than a dozen books and had his eyes and ears open, does not understand a few basic things about the phenomenon. Nevertheless, a very large number of students seem to know startlingly little about the anatomy of violence. Some of them have learned—the hard way; others, I suspect, will learn that way in the future. A little thought on the subject, however, might prevent a lot of pain.

Given certain ingredients, it is as nearly impossible to be a "little bit violent" as it is to be "a little bit pregnant." Once started, the thing is going to run its course—full term. Man, as an individual, has one thing in common with certain animals (the grizzly bear being a notable one), an immensely explosive "something" in his nature. It is imperfectly understood by psychiatrists, but I suspect that most of them, Freudian and otherwise, would agree that while man has essentially the same adrenal, nervous and muscular systems as his fellow mammals, the development of his brain has been such that a tight lid is placed on instinctual drives and on such conduct as would greatly release internal pressures but is forbidden by mores, rules, laws or by rationality itself.

I don't know enough psychological jargon to expand on this theme, nor, I think, need I do so. It is obvious to anyone who takes a look at himself, to say nothing of his friends and enemies, that there is a "pent-up" aspect to man's nature which is present in few, if any, of his mammalian cousins. It varies, of course, from man to man but it is there—always there.

Ordinarily, man keeps himself under tight control, but there are times when he does not. One of those times is when he becomes a lost integer in a mob. There *is* such a thing as a mob psychology—and people caught up in it go wild. They are then capable of acts of wanton viciousness of which they would never be guilty in an individually rational sense.

Even wan and peaceful Linda Eldredge, in her *Time* magazine essay, said, "Violence? I abhor it . . . and condemn it." Yet one short paragraph previously, peace-loving, weary little Linda had written, "You throw a bottle and it feels good. You say F - - - and it feels good. If you can't change it, blow it up. It becomes a very personal and illogical thing."

Indeed it does, it becomes a mob and in a mob a man

becomes a beast. And he remains a beast either until he meets a physical force superior to his own or until exhaustion overcomes him. History is far too replete with incidents of mob action to pursue the subject by extracting examples. But mob violence has these common ingredients: Its contagion, charged with emotionalism of extremely high voltage, converts a decent, rational man into a wildly aggressive animal. He can and does become a murderer, an arsonist, a vandal and a mindless instrument of destruction. A mob is engaging, utterly without rationality, in a gigantic mass cathartic. Its explosive energy can almost never be channeled or checked. It is as apt to turn in upon itself as outward toward others. It sucks innocent people into its vortex and it respects no one or anything.

Among the American citizenry there is a group which understands this wildness, a group which knows full well how terribly dangerous a mob can be. This group consists of riot police, military forces suddenly called to riot duty and, understandably, people who themselves have been in previous riots—people who have been in the mob.

There is an axiom among those (and they are far too few in number) who have undergone thorough training in riot control: "Use minimum force to overcome force." That process has about as much overall validity to it as the military axiom: "The best defense is a good offense." Sometimes so, sometimes not. The fact remains that in dealing with rioters the forces of law are confronting an enormously dangerous, mindless beast. And the fact remains, irrespective of training, that if campus riots continue, it will not be four dead students at Kent State, it will be dozens and then hundreds—most of them probably innocent. And whatever happens, the cry of "Police Brutality" will inevitably ring out.

The University of Wisconsin, in the last of a series of violent events, literally blew sky-high. Early in September 1970, Sterling Hall was blown up by a bomb which killed Physicist Robert E. Fassnacht, destroyed the life work of at least five physics professors and the doctoral research of two dozen graduate students. It destroyed a $500,000 computer and did perhaps another million dollars' worth of additional damage. Why? Because, said the radicals who claimed responsibility (the New Year's Gang), the center for military research was Sterling Hall and "By ignoring reasoned argument and negotiation the university's managers provoked rebellion." It was that simple! Was it that simple to physicist Fassnacht who, as his father said, "was sympathetic to many of the discontents here on campus"? The day following the explosion the "New Year's Gang" issued an unbelievably petulant broadside, not only justifying the bombing but threatening more explosions unless a list of absurd demands were met by October thirtieth.

But this was only the last of many incidents on that beleaguered campus. The trouble started when students protested the presence of a Dow Chemical Company representative as a recruiter on campus in October 1968. It flared quickly, and in a very short time students were swarming around the building in which the recruiter was conducting interviews. About 100 protestors blocked the door of the room in which he was operating. Another 2000 students, in an obviously ugly mood, chanting, shouting and threatening, milled outside. Entered now *thirty,* repeat *thirty,* Madison police. They arrived on the scene a few at a time. Some came in their private automobiles; some had riot helmets, some did not. They assembled (and remember the odds, roughly 30 to 2000) tried to enter the building and were thrown back. One officer was hit in the face with a brick, which broke his nose.

One account, highly critical of the police, reported that the "police used their nightsticks freely" (I would hope so; what were they supposed to use, rubber tomahawks?). Nightsticks or no, this group of policemen was now being pelted with stones, bricks, bottles, shoes—and even with their own nightsticks.[3] The police van was first blocked and then disabled. The county sheriff's office sent reinforcements and in due course this pitifully small force dispersed the mob. Some fifty students were injured, and about twenty police were also injured, three of them "seriously and suffering permanent damage." Why no deaths? Luck and uncommon, almost incredible, police restraint. But in the course of events like this one, luck and restraint do not emerge from a deep reservoir, but from a very shallow one. Almost invariably law enforcement contingents on campuses are grossly outnumbered. They are human, however well trained; they are armed with handguns as well as nightsticks. The time will come when they will use handguns—and in unison—because they will have to and they may well have to do so, depending on the circumstances, within the confines of the "minimum force" axiom.

There is another group of people who thoroughly understand the mob, its deadliness, its mindlessness. They are the student activists; they are the firebrand militants, the violent ones. They not only understand it, they set the stage for it, they use the bullhorn rhetoric, they print and disperse the pamphlets, they start and feed the rumors, they seize the issue (or invent one). They point the way. They understand full well that once they can raise a fever pitch of emotion, it takes but one cry, one shouted instruction and one pointed

---

[3] See *Protest, op. cit.,* p. 258.

finger to explode the situation. And they have been busy long
before the issue has been "chosen." They have made the
bombs—and they have even hooked in the little Linda Eldredge who nonetheless in *Time* writes, "We feel horror at
death and find ourselves planning it in Weatherman base-
ments." They hook in also, not only the naïve and confused,
like Linda, but the true paranoids—of which there is always
a handy percentage in *any* group of thousands.

"But," I have heard it said until it nauseates me, "universities must reform—and the violence occurs because they
haven't and won't." Just for a moment let us view that senti-
ment in the light of what happened at San Francisco State
College, one of the most torn, beleaguered and ravaged
schools in America.

San Francisco State, one of the largest of the eighteen state
colleges in California, was, before its nightmare began, one
of the finest schools of its kind in America. It had an unusually distinguished faculty. As of 1966, its president, John
H. Summerskill, was young, liberal, unusually sensitive to
the problems and hopes of students—especially from minority
ethnic groups. It was a proudly open campus; its faculty senate was the first in America to seat students as voting members; it was the birthplace of the country's first student-run
experimental college; it was one of the nation's first schools
to set up a black studies program; it was one of the first
to terminate a contract with ROTC. San Francisco State, in
other words, was in the vanguard of liberal, open, experi-
menting, innovative institutions in America.

If, then, the object of confrontation and violence on the
campus is reform, why has San Francisco State been the most
disrupted college in America? If the SDS, the Third World
Liberation Front and a dozen other *ad hoc* groups were after

reform, why *destroy* the school which probably promised more in the way of reform than any other college?

The answer is, of course, that the violent ones are not the least interested in reform. They are interested in destruction, not only of the university, but of all American institutions and structures. Are they, then, true revolutionaries in the classic sense of the term? No. A revolutionary wants to destroy the extant structure because he has a better one in mind. A revolutionary has a clearly defined (usually a very elaborately and philosophically defined) "in lieu of" system. He has classically been, therefore, a careful, even a meticulous planner. And, more importantly, his attack on the status quo has almost always been launched precisely from the platform (on a comparative basis) of his "in lieu of" system. Moreover, most revolutionaries have clearly understood the anatomy of revolution—and the odds for and against success. They have been good politicians, knowing that power flows only from certain combinations and alliances and from class patterns and coalitions.

Today's violent ones are anything but revolutionaries in any accurate sense of the word. They have in no sense articulated an "in lieu of" system or structure. They show utterly no understanding of present American social, political or economic structures. They hate them, but they have negligible knowledge of how they work or don't work or what coalitions keep the system together. If they *did* have that knowledge they would stop calling themselves "revolutionaries" and invent some other terms for their activities, because even a primer knowledge of elementary extent would reveal that the ingredients for revolution in America in the foreseeable future are simply nonexistent. Trouble? Yes, all kinds of it. Revolution? No.

Well, then, who are the violent ones and why are they that way and what do they hope to accomplish? The latter question first. They hope, with enormous egocentrism, to accomplish precisely what they are accomplishing: to involve themselves in an almost orgiastic series of violent events which permit them, however momentarily, a place in the sun. They are not interested in ends because it is only the means that satisfy them. They can crawl for that brief moment up out of the misery of self-obsession and self-hate, up out of the dark hole of their own fear and for that moment feel alive and powerful. Are they then *sick?* Yes, which is one of the reasons they are so hard to deal with. Is their activity dissent? No. Many, many students on *most* campuses are dissenting and vehemently. But not these, not the violent ones. A good many of them don't even bother to rationalize what they are doing as dissent. How and why did they get that way?

If you turned one hundred of America's most prestigious psychiatrists loose on one thousand of the violent ones and gave them five years to probe their subjects, I suspect an answer that approached the definitive might emerge. But that is unlikely to happen, so let me *suggest* why the violent ones are the way they are. One key lies in their own vocabulary: "nonnegotiable demands"; "gut reaction"; "cooptation"; "now"; "relevant."

One scholar who has studied the activists, Dr. Ralph M. Goldman, Professor of Political Science at San Francisco State (a good field laboratory if ever there was one), has even broken the activists' word "confrontation" down into its working parts, i.e., instant majoritarianism—which simply means that a minority does (via TV or whatever devices it can use) everything that it can to *appear* to be a majority.

Dr. Goldman goes on with "instant equality," which simply

means that, again, via TV, newspaper coverage, and other media, the militant seeks to shunt offstage all parties to the conflict other than his own. At the very least, he seeks "equality" with a second party only—so that, for instance, all gray is abolished and the conflict is reduced to black and white. As Goldman puts it, "A pitched battle with the cops is always productive of Instant Equality."[4] The students then become the "good guys" and the police the Fascist Pig "bad guys." There are other Goldman breakdowns of the working parts of "confrontation," but these two examples are sufficient.

What is involved in all these phrases and the context in which they are used is "now"—we want what we want "now." We will not negotiate, we will not wait, we will not reason (gut reaction), we will not discuss, we will not communicate, we will not compromise. We want it all and we want it now.

If you draw that picture of the violent ones and then think about it for a moment, almost inevitably it conjures up the picture of an infant—an overgrown, articulate infant, but an infant in all his essential responses nonetheless. Ask and it shall be given ye, and it it isn't, throw a tantrum and *then* it shall be given ye. If you don't like the oatmeal, throw it on the floor.

Behind the violent one, whatever the nuances of variation in his background, there lies this fact. He got too much, too soon, too easily in his life. Call it overindulgence, call it permissiveness, call it what you will, the product is an egocentric boor, an enormously self-centered, terribly spoiled, fearfully unfulfilled (precisely because he has been overfilled) brat.

Since for all the years of his life, up until the time he erupts on some campus, he has gotten what he wanted either by

---

[4] See *Dissent,* May, 1968, or, for another version, *Protest, op. cit.,* p. 271.

threatening violence or by being violent, why not now? It is a conditioned reflex.

Is that too simple an explanation for the phenomenon? Yes, doubtless there are other elements—and in each and every family from which a violent one sprang, more and varied aberrancies in backgrounds.

There is a point of near congruence in all the numerous studies of dissenters and activists (*not necessarily violent*) which have flooded the market of late, and that is that they come from upper-middle-class backgrounds and from families with higher incomes, on the average, than nonactivists. Their parents tend to be markedly liberal. They tend to have higher IQ's and get better grades than the nonactivists. Their parents tend to be above average both in formal education and in intellectual interests. None of which casts any light on whether those parents have *also* been grossly permissive. It is my own very limited personal experience with the breed, however, that they are *precisely* those given to overindulgence and permissiveness.

But let us assume for a moment that my generation, in large part, *has* been overindulgent and permissive. Let us even assume that that is one of my generation's salient character-istics. Why, then, if the root explanation for the violent ones is overindulgence and permissiveness, are the violent ones so few? Why have we not produced a whole generation of egocentric, spoiled slobs?

Many American eighteen-year-olds don't go to college. They marry and go to work and have children. The world is funny that way. It does not respond to "I want it and I want it now." Instead, it kicks you in the teeth and the boss says, "You're fired."

Many of these non-college youths are drafted and the army

is funny that way. It puts you on KP or throws you in the brig; it cuts off your hair and makes you run 20 miles with a full pack. Retribution? Torture? No, just the army. So the average American non-college youth, however indulged, simply bumps into the real world—and that, in whatever form, is a most chastening experience. The young man who decides that he can run the railroad better than the president is shortly persuaded that that is not the case. On the other hand, the young man in college who decides that he can run the university better than the president is sometimes led to believe that that may, indeed, be the case.

So there are two worlds for the younger generation—the non-college and the college. The latter, with its freedom, with its former *in loco parentis* role now gone, with its lack of structure in the form of a real chain of command, is grist for the mill of the violent one. Here and only here he can use the very freedom he has to abuse it; here and only here he can *say* that what he is does rise out of his idealism; here and only here will his elders (the faculty) not only listen, but often listen sympathetically. Here and only here is he in large part immune from the outrage of the community that otherwise would simply ostracize him.

But, you say, there are still 7,000,000 youths on our campuses and the violent ones constitute a tiny minority. If the general overindulgence and permissiveness of the average American family is truly a basic cause in the production of the violent ones, why are they so few? Well, in spite of factors mitigating against maturity, maturity often still occurs because it is in the nature of man to mature with his years. Most do, a few don't. Is it that simple? Probably not. There are vast differences in people from similar, if not identical, backgrounds. Each of my own seven children differs greatly from the others. Genes? Luck? A turn of events? Fortuity? I don't know. But whatever accounts for the common sense, civility, decency, and fine character of the vast majority of college students in America today, I am profoundly grateful.

In one form or another a large portion of these 7,000,000 students are today dissenting. Thank God. It is in that dissent, against senseless war, against environmental degradation, against poverty and injustice that reform lies. So long—and just so long—as it is not turned from its myriad proper channels (and they *are* myriad) into the channels of the violent ones. That way lies suppression, terrible disillusionment and, in the end, the failure of America.

Another word, then, about the violent ones: If they are so few, why do they wield such power? I have explained that partly on the basis of the fragility of the university. But there is more to it than that.

They have power also because they are listened to by people who should know better. For want of a better word, a new word, they are listened to by "liberal" administrations and faculties. And they are listened to because the "liberal" has become a very confused man.

The worst violence, the greatest damage to true liberalism, has occurred at the most "liberal" schools—the freest, the most open. John Summerskill and his successor, Robert Smith, were among the most liberal of college presidents. Take a look at San Francisco State today. They, like dozens of their kind, believed that minor conflicts on campus could always be headed off from becoming major conflicts and prolonged confrontation, provided only that the administration and faculty remained sympathetic and responsive even in the face of extreme provocation. At "liberal" school after school, it did not work. The latest bombing at the University of Wisconsin at Madison took one life, but bombings had become routine at San Francisco State, the College of San Mateo, Berkeley, Wisconsin State at Oshkosh, and elsewhere. The "liberal" president of Swarthmore died of a heart attack while trying to "reason" with students who were occupying buildings. And then the most "liberal" and open of them all blew up—Harvard.

The liberal faculty member's confusion seems to lie in his inability to distinguish between rationally rooted dissent and egocentric authoritarianism. He seems unable to spot that point where the one crosses over into the other. If the liberal in America is anything, he is a man who has had faith in *institutions* to function within a democratic society. When he participates, therefore, in a process aimed at destroying those institutions—what happened to his liberalism?

Nathan Glazer is a sociologist at Berkeley—and a liberal. Glazer sees the point well enough. He understands that the real liberal simply cannot attribute all current problems to self-interested misuse of power, because, as he puts it, "there can be no substitute for institutions, even though they may become tired, bureaucratic and corrupt."[5] Knowing this, the "liberals' " support of the nebulous, vague and essentially non-sensical substitute "participatory democracy" is not liberal but essentially anarchic.

But more puzzling still is the liberal's fascination with the rhetoric of the student militant when it is usually clearly elitist and anything but egalitarian—and when, indeed, the far left is much closer to the far right than to any position which might be termed "liberal." The aim of both far left and far right is the absolute dominance by a minority over a majority. A "liberal" view?

Liberals readily understand the utter necessity of dissent

---

[5] See *Protest, op. cit.,* p. 43.

in a society like our own, and the need for reform on dozens of fronts, but what a great many of them fail to understand is that the means adopted by the radicals whom they too often join are precisely those most calculated to undermine the concepts of freedom and democracy so dear to the liberal heart. It is ardently to be hoped that the academic liberal will, and soon, withdraw his support from the violent ones and rediscover the real precepts of liberalism.

One last word on the inordinate power of the violent ones. They are operating in a general milieu of dissent, mixed up with the uncommitted ones, the standers-by, the waiters-to-see. This is a fertile culture for their yeast. Unless the majority of students come fairly soon to see that it is *their* buildings that are being burned, that it is *their* education that is being disrupted, and above all, that it is their future which campus violence is jeopardizing (not mine), the game can be lost.

In the end, the most effective way of handling the violent ones is for the great mass of students to say *no*! It is for them to say, "We see you now for what you are and what you are attacking. You are not attacking war, injustice, corruption, poverty, blight. You are attacking *us*."

When students themselves across the land on all the campuses come to see this for the truth it is—it will be all over for the violent ones. All over—and very quickly and very quietly. For the nonviolent students themselves are the real meat upon which the violent ones are feeding.

Chapter 5

And the Older Generation

Periodically the world gets in a mess. In fact, it is most unusual for it *not* to be in a mess. The normal state of affairs is not peace, it is war of one kind or another, or a series of conditions fraught with the possibilities, if not the probabilities, of war, or a peace so uneasy as really not to be peace at all.

Nor, indeed, has war been mankind's only scourge. Hunger, disease, deprivation, plague, lawlessness, slavery, injustice, cruel totalitarianism, genocide, what have you, have often been more generally applicable to man's condition than has peace, joy, justice, health, freedom and general well-being.

But in the past, even within the confines of one nation, the United States, say, misery existed in pockets separated by pockets—by distance, topography and by the ponderously slow methods by which the word spread from place to place. Moreover, when finally it did spread, by word of mouth, by letter—and far, far later by telegraph—the event (the crime, the flood, the battle) was over. It was not only far away, it was long ago. The fierce impact of it was lost in time and distance.

That no longer being true, the world not only seems to be in more of a mess than it has ever been before, the nature of the mess seems new, and that which is actually very old and cumulative seems suddenly to burst upon one's consciousness, veritably into the living room or the bedroom, as some new horror, apocalyptic and fearsome.

It is obvious to me now, though somehow I missed the point at the time, that as I climbed aboard the train to set off for basic training for World War II, and as I shook my father's hand, I should have said to him, "If your goddam blind generation had not lost the peace after World War I, if your stupid senators had not frustrated Wilson, Adolf Hitler would never have come to power and I would not now be going off to war." But of course I was improperly conditioned.

Long before that, when I was nine years old, I should have told my father, "Don't whine to me about Black Friday and the fact that we have lost our shirts. If your goddam generation hadn't gone into an insane speculative frenzy and hadn't been so goddam greedy to make a quick buck (while you were dancing your crazy Charleston and drinking illegal booze) I wouldn't have to suffer now through your Depression—holes in my shoes, beans instead of beef and no money for a haircut."

When, much later, the Navy wrote me to stand by for recall for the Korean War (I was not called), I should have handed the letter to my father and said, "If your knuckle-headed President and your blind diplomats had had the sense to read up a little on the Far East and had been tending to the proper priorities at home, I wouldn't have to be going off to fight another war for you."

The fact is that all through the years of my life until I was thirty, I utterly failed to point out to my elders how great a proportion of my time up to that point had been spent in dealing with the problems *they* had created for me. The fact is that that is literally true and that I did suffer from my father's generation's mistakes. And he from his father's, and he from his, ad infinitum.

I did not spend my time blaming my father's generation for the world they had left me for two very basic reasons: First, though he was a kind and understanding man, he would have picked me up by the seat of the pants and the scruff of the neck and thrown me out the door. Second, there being no television, I occasionally read books and certainly by the time I was in my early teens I had *some* notion that man had an imperfect nature and that as events built up on events, an accumulation of the past always afflicts the present. Always has and always will. Depending on the accumulation, every generation spends a goodly portion of its time dealing with inherited problems and suffering from inherited mistakes. The rest of its time it divides between dealing with its own mistakes and making progress. So, in effect, each generation's time is apportioned three ways: time to deal with its inherited problems, time to deal with the problems it creates for itself, and time to step out and do some good things. The apportionment varies from generation to generation.

The fact that bright young men (like my nephew) in the fullness of their years should complain so incessantly and so early about my generation's mistakes is simply a grave waste of time because it detracts from the time they have for the other categories of apportionment—including the time to make their own mistakes.

Moreover, there are degrees of the longevity of generational mistakes, depending, of course, on the seriousness of the mistake. For instance, the generation which came into its full power in the 1850's was unable to solve a grave social, moral, economic and political problem: slavery. True, it had inherited this problem from an earlier generation that had, in the first instance, instituted slavery. Nonetheless, and complex as the problem was, the generation of the 1850's failed to solve it. The result was not only one of history's bloodiest wars, the results reverberated down the corridors of the country's time from that day to this.

The younger generation, in addition to incessantly blaming my generation for the mistakes it *has* made, telescopes time and blames us for those visited upon us by our predecessors. Among the other weird consequences of their obsession for "blaming," plus this phenomenon of "telescoping," is that they blame us more readily for our accomplishments than for our genuine mistakes.

My generation, for instance, is constantly accused of being "racist." To be sure, there are racists among us, just as there have been racists in all generations that preceded us. The cold, hard, demonstrable fact remains that my generation has done more to end racism in America than all others combined; the fact is that this is true not only in the light of Supreme Court decisions, statutes and *de jure* activities, it is also true *de facto*. The black man in America has made giant strides forward in all realms and all areas and has done so under the aegis, concern, demands and attitudes of *my* generation. The fact is that my generation is the only one to have tackled this problem head-on, *de jure* and *de facto* in the history of America—and it has done so more aggressively than any generation in the history of the world (among those nations with racial problems of consequence).

Does the black man now enjoy the equality, the justice, the political and economic power he deserves? Of course not.

Have there been setbacks? Of course. But it is patently absurd of the younger generation not to recognize enormous progress when they see it and it goes beyond absurdity to accuse us of causing the black's degradation in the first place. It will be an accomplishment of extraordinary proportions if they (the younger generation) can keep up the pace of progress when their time comes. Most certainly they will not do so if a significant proportion of them keep blaming and telescoping. Nor will they accomplish much unless they come finally to understand that to undo more than 300 years of deep-seated racial animosity and suppression will take more than loose-jointed rhetoric and black studies programs.

I have alluded to environmental degradation before, but as an example of "telescoping" it deserves a few more comments. Here, again, the finger of blame is pointed at the *only* generation that has faced up to and aggressively attacked a problem of long standing. It is entirely true that the technological explosion following World War II exacerbated an already bad situation—and it is entirely true that my generation presided over that explosion (a development which, in general, I applaud). But before my generation took up the cry, not one in ten thousand Americans had ever heard the word ecology. Before my generation, nobody gave a damn about the quality of air and water, and no one had even bothered to create devices to measure the extent of air and water contamination.

In 1930, 1600 people dropped dead in Liège, Belgium, due to a weather inversion, and the effluent from an aluminum plant. And they buried their dead and wept and went back to work.

One man in my own home state (Montana) described the mining city of Butte in 1871 thus: "On a windless day the smoke lay so heavy at mid-day that lamps were burned and thieves were as fearless at noon as at midnight." London's famous Sherlock-Holmes-fog wasn't fog, it was smog. European cities underwent periodic pollution catastrophes in the nineteenth century—and no one did a thing about it.

The scientists now so busily at work both in the laboratories and in the field, the scientists who have learned to measure, and in many instances to control many thousands of kinds of pollutants, are of my generation. The enormous public campaigns to clean up the air, the water and the land were designed, launched and are sustained by my generation. The television specials designed to make every American man, woman and child conscious of the dangers to the ecosystem are written, produced and paid for by my generation. The swarm of lawsuits filed by swarms of environmental groups all represent my generation. The statutes, laws and rulings aimed at creating a clean environment emanate from my generation's legislators, lawyers and judges.

Again, the younger generation will have accomplished a feat of great proportion if they can keep up the pace of progress when their time comes. But, also, again, if too large a percentage of them think that they can do it with ragtag rhetoric or if they think that they can clean up in two weeks what it took a couple of hundred years to make dirty—they will do far less than we have done even to date. And we are far from through.

You, they say—or a very great many of them say—have blighted our lives with an illegal war in Vietnam. Well, we are in a war in Vietnam, and we stumbled and bumbled our way into it—and it was a mistake. And we are getting out of it. Hindsight is a wonderful thing. A great many very well-informed, thoroughly decent, very thoughtful Americans thought that what we were doing was right and necessary and moral. In my own mind, events have proven that they were wrong. Those in positions of great power and hence of great responsibility miscalculated. The miscalculations were grievous. You, the younger generation, *are* suffering for it. So are we. So am I; I have a son in South Korea. Go ahead, then, indict us for those blunders. We are not whining nor self-flagellating. We *are* indicting ourselves. But bear this in mind when you are balancing the scales.

There was another war once and probably the only reason you are here at all, let alone free to indict anyone, is that we fought it and won it. Sixteen million young Americans were in uniform in World War II; 291,000 were killed, and 670,000 were wounded. It lasted six long, painful and bitter years. And except that it made it possible for there to be another generation of free Americans, those years were irretrievably lost to the majority of my generation. There were sixteen million of us under arms—and that is a lot of lost years. And they were lost to my generation, not to yours.

My generation *has* presided over what has been the fastest and most comprehensive technological development in man's history. Technology has become a very bad word because its spin-off has created some severe problems and these have been seized upon by too many of the pontificating young as absolute indicators of the dehumanization of man. So often, so repetitiously, so vehemently, has the word been misused and the process misunderstood, that it now conjures up in the mind only congeries of terrible machines doing terrible things at a terrible pace to a helpless society. The litany is a song with one perpetual sour note, a ceaseless beating on a single drum and a witless chant.

To deal merely with the medical aspects of technological

advances under the aegis of my generation would take volumes. Those advances (and they are *technological*) have so reduced age-old human suffering that it beggars the mind. To chronicle the pharmaceutical wonders alone would take more volumes. And further volumes would be required to describe how vastly the *machines* of medicine have alleviated suffering. The lives saved by the *technology* of medicine, by the blinking, whirring *machines* of medicine are uncountable. The kidney machine, the heart-lung machine, the pacemaker, aluminum hip joints, cardiographs, encephalographs, liver scanners, artery catheters, proctoscopes—machine after machine after machine has been an almost indescribable boon to mankind. This too is technology. And in the long history of medical advances, those which have taken place under the technological genius of my generation, far, far outpace that of any other generation.

There is constant talk today about the population explosion and the dangers inherent in it. What generation produced the birth control pill? But far more significantly, what nation and what generation through *technological* developments has made it possible for Barbara Ward to say, "Mankind has the chance over the next two decades of reversing the present trend toward catastrophe . . . the hope lies in the Green Revolution, the new farm *technology* [italics mine] based on hybrids, water and fertilizer which can double and treble food and work for the world's developing peoples."[1]

Lester R. Brown, Senior Fellow in the Overseas Development Council, and leading authority on "the Green Revolu-

_____

[1] See Lester R. Brown, *Seeds of Change: The Green Revolution and Development in the 1970's* (New York: Praeger, 1970), p. 206.

tion," says of this technological breakthrough, "It promises to improve the well-being of more people in a shorter time than any other single technological advance in history."[2] The simple fact is that these technological advances in new, enormously productive seed hybrids and new techniques of cultivation constitute (not in the distant future, but in the very near future) the opportunity to eliminate almost all hunger in the world! And the older, not the younger, generation did it.

Certainly technology is a two-edged sword. Certainly as it solves some problems it creates others, but on balance to assert that technological development is dehumanizing mankind and that it has done so largely due to the older generation's mishandling of it is not merely the product of dim vision, it may also be the product of a dim wit.

But, then, the vision of a number of young people *is* dim; dim looking forward and dimmer looking backward. How many of them know, for instance, that when my generation finished fighting World War II, it not only lifted up and reconstituted its allies, but its enemies as well? For self-interest only? Poppycock! There was a deep humanitarianism in the Marshall Plan. For self-interest only? It is hardly self-interest to pile heavy new taxes on yourself year after year to help Frenchmen and Englishmen and Germans and Japanese. The younger generation talks a great deal about loving one's fellow man. They have more than a pocketful of clichés to pull out for the occasion. It is a good deal cheaper to pass out flowers and talk about loving one's fellow man than to dig in where it hurts and rebuild its ravaged society, feeding its kids, holding up its morale and paying its bills. But we did precisely

---

[2] *Ibid.,* p. 196.

that—and nothing like it had ever been done before by any generation.

What most irritates me, however, is this business of "nowness." It irritates me because I think it accounts in large part for the dim vision—which is really just another way of saying "lack of faith." I don't think that my generation, ripped and torn from the beginning as it was, ever developed the *static* sense that seems to beset so many of today's young people. "What is always will be." But the order of things is change. My generation knew that. This new one seems not to. If you are constantly preoccupied with "now," *of course* things seem static. If you look behind and ahead of you, you quickly recognize that the order of things *is* change. And you have to recognize that fact before you can see the potential in it—which may be why we have so many young people who seem to lack faith that the future will be any different from the past. It will be different, whether they wish it or not, but there is no guarantee that the change will be for the better unless they seek aggressively to make it so.

Nor am I much taken with the younger generation's negligible recognition of what "society" is. They use the word pejoratively, but very often indeed, they don't know what the words mean—nor why, when challenged—society reacts hostilely.

I have a young friend, a very hippie girl, about eighteen, with a young, very hippie boyfriend, about twenty-one. They are, in fact when you get to know them, nice, bright young people. She wears an old buffalo coat, her hair is straggly. She wears granny glasses (with no lenses) and either sandals or a weird kind of built-up boot, the kind one sees on a club-footed person.

The boyfriend has very long, thin, wispy hair and wears

the usual conglomerate hippie apparel, spotted pants, beads and sandals, belts, sashes and a headband.

Last summer they decided to hitchhike through Mexico. First of all, they were peremptorily turned back at the border. Secondly, in hitchhiking from Montana to the Mexican border and back, they encountered a series of "affronts" the most serious of which was that they were refused service in perhaps a half dozen restaurants.

When they returned to the university I had a long talk with them. They were bitterly resentful that they had not been permitted to enter Mexico and the girl, staring at me with a brooding resentment, said, "You call this a free country. Well, we did not find it so. [Incidentally, it was Mexico that denied them entry.] A free country doesn't treat people the way we were treated. Restaurants in free countries don't throw people out simply because they don't wear shoes or comb their hair." I didn't argue much. I think I clucked my sympathy and let it go at that.

But I did not forget the incident because since then, in talking to dozens of young "nonconformists" (a very silly term since what they are is rigidly conformist in dress, thought, speech and mores), I have found this same resentment, this same sullen belief that "society" is rigidly stratified, unyielding and "against" them. And I always find behind the sullenness a sort of grim pleasure in being martyred.

I finally asked one young hippie if he had ever seen a porcupine. He avowed that he had, indeed. I asked him what a porcupine did when you poked him with a stick. He replied, "Well, he curls up into a spiny ball and lashes his tail at you." And I said, "Well, that is what society does when you poke it with a stick." But he saw no connection—and that was that.

But there *is* a connection. Society, *any* society, will act very quickly to protect itself from what is strange to it, foreign to it, and perhaps dangerous to it.

Deep in the mind, or perhaps in the viscera, of every man lies the recognition of the fact that without society—without that "something" of which he is an integral part, without its order, its rules, without commonality, he is lost. Man is a herd animal, a social animal, a gregarious mammal. He cannot live without society, of whatever kind, without the rules for conduct which protect *him*. He may know this only instinctively, but he knows it, and knowing, he will react, along with his kind (a vast majority in any relatively stable society) with quick and positive alarm to any intrusion. The porcupine.

Another bearded, bead-bedecked hippie, when I referred later to society's "porcupine reaction," said, "Well, I was born a century too late. The Indian way of life, freedom on the high plains in unspoiled country. Those people *really* had it. That is the freedom we have lost."

I informed him that in my view it was vastly better that he had *not* been born an Indian a century earlier, because Indian rules and societal regulations were extraordinarily tough and rigid and that the punishment for the violation of these rules was often extraordinarily cruel. I averred that a hippie in that society would not be merely sneered at, but that he would at the very least be whipped. More probably he would be banished—which usually meant death. I told him that whatever he thought of American society, and however resentful he might be toward those who sneered at his hair and dress, very few societies in the world today or in the societies of the past would permit such aberrance at all. Maybe, just maybe, he was born in the only society at the only time that would permit him to be what he was and do what he did—and confine itself to occasional sneers.

To the rejoinder that hair and beards and clothes do not reveal the inner man, that they are not dangerous, that they do not constitute a threat to society, I can only agree. But they are a symbolic attack on mores and customs having to do with deportment—of which dress is a part. They constitute the stick poked at the porcupine. If you don't mind the reaction of the porcupine, go ahead and do and be what you wish.

An inordinate number of young people exhibit contempt for politics and politicians. At student function after function this spring, summer and fall, the word "politics" or "politician" has brought forth derisive catcalls, booing and hissing, as if, indeed, the political process and its professional "practitioners" were fools—or worse, blithering agents of the conspiracy to "do in" the young. This puzzled me for some time until, through interviews and discussions, I discerned the reason.

A great many young people have a grossly simplistic view of politics and, worse, they do not understand that the process works (and has been productive of enormous freedom for many generations of Americans) because at the core of it is compromise. And this, for entirely too many of the younger generation, constitutes a process (compromise) that they do not understand. You cannot see the virtue in compromise, of course, if you believe yourself to be the sole possessor of the right and the true. You cannot see the value (indeed, the necessity) of compromise unless you can also see that your antagonist is as honest as you are in seeking solutions to problems, and that methodology and means are far more often involved than ends.

This *attitude* is not due to the inadequacies of civics text-books and civics teachers. They have always dealt more with the ideal of politics than the real because the intricacies of the real are practically impossible to teach in a quarter or a semester. The attitude is due, I think, much more to the youthful conviction that they and they alone possess the truth—they and they alone are right. In light of that arrogance, compromise becomes a retreat from high principle, and thus those who advocate compromise (politicians) become knaves.

The pity of this is that there are now 31,000,000 Americans between the ages of twenty-one and thirty and that constitutes an enormous power which could readily be applied to the polls. Moreover, if the new eighteen-year-old voting bill survives the test of constitutionality, it will add eleven million more to the voting roles. As former Chief Justice Warren put it, "Youth has the voting power to lead a crusade whenever it wishes to do so." Yet it will not do so and cannot do so if it spurns this power as somehow unclean and unworthy of its high endeavor.

Closely allied to this contempt for politics is the "frustration syndrome." It is sufficiently widespread and monotonously asserted to be an endemic condition among the young.

A few months ago, due to my initial letter to my brother and the unusual nationwide response, I appeared on the "Life with Linkletter" show, a somewhat harrowing but interesting experience. During the show I was questioned by a number of students in the audience, very bright and, I thought, very well coached. All of them, in one form or another, expressed *frustration*. One pretty young coed asked, in effect, "We are so *frustrated*. You do not have to suffer that affliction. What can we do about our frustration?" I forget what I answered, except that it wasn't a very good answer.

What I should have done was point to Art Linkletter and say, "Do you think *he* isn't frustrated? Yet what an active and exciting life he leads!" What I should have said was, *"Everyone* is frustrated because no one becomes all of what he wants to be. No one lives up to the potential he feels within himself. Certainly, the degree varies from man to man and woman to woman. But we are *all* frustrated to some degree in our marriages, in our jobs, in our hopes for ourselves and our families, and in our hopes for mankind and the world."

I should have told the young lady, "Live with your frustration, learn to understand it, learn to *compromise* with what you want to be and what you are, with what you want to do and what you can do. That is growing up; that is maturity—and there is no way on God's green earth to get there unless you understand compromise—when to use it and when not."

Still, the frustration, the sullenness and the resentment are there. They are there because a very large number of young people have not come to grips with themselves within the very real and hard perimeters that life has set for them. And these negative qualities are there because a great many young people do not know why "society," in whatever form, is so vital and necessary for its members. Nor do many of them know that if they destroy *this* society and its structures, they will merely get another in its stead—with this difference: There is not one chance in ten million that it will be less suppressive and more open than the society they now condemn.

Flawed as it is, calcified where it is calcified, corrupt where it is corrupt, out of balance where it is off-center, the road to greater freedom, to greater openness is the peaceful and thoughtful reform of what we have, not its violent destruction for some "in lieu of" something. My generation knows that. We have always known it. The question is, Does the younger generation know it—and if they do, will they join us; or, in time, because they do not think enough, or see clearly enough, will they let the violent ones determine the matter for them?

Chapter 6

Student Problems and the Law

A FEW years ago, I met a friend of mine coming out of the county courthouse. He looked dejected and confused. When I asked him what the trouble was, he said that he had just lost a lawsuit (civil) and that he simply couldn't understand how he could have lost it. "The law," he said, "just doesn't bear any relationship to common sense."

Often it doesn't seem to. It is built, in a rough way, on precedent. It is organic. If, indeed, you could take a motion picture of it as an "entity," it would look something like an amoeba, bulging here, narrowing there, moving forward, reversing course and generally moving in many directions at the same time—without ever quite coming apart. Precedent, as an invariable rule, simply isn't invariable; courts are constantly overthrowing it, reversing themselves and establishing new precedents for old.

The president of a very prominent West Coast university responded with weary resignation to a recent article of mine in which I advocated a much wider use of expulsion as a device to keep order on campuses. He stated that I did not understand "due process," and that it was much more difficult to expel a student than I thought. He remarked that the courts, at least in his state, had in recent years so tightened up their procedures that to expel a student had become a most difficult operation.

It is certainly true that many university administrators are utterly confused about what they may or may not do in terms of disciplinary action with respect to disruptive students. It is true that the law is in a state of swift flux on the issue, and that what may or may not be done varies from place to place and time to time.

In its most recent booklet on the civil liberties of students in colleges and universities,[1] the American Civil Liberties Union concluded: "Constitutional law regarding student rights is now in a rapid state of flux. . . . It will be wise, therefore, in the near future, not only to keep one moistened finger on the pages of precedent, but to keep another pointed toward the strong winds of change."

No doubt. But in the meantime, university administrators cannot sit around listening to lawyers argue while the building is burning down around them; nor, paralyzed by the convolutions of legal phraseology, can they (as they all too often have) assume that the entry of "due process" onto the campus scene prevents them from taking fast, affirmative disciplinary action (meaning mainly expulsion) in the case of riotous student activists.

The simple fact is that there is a substantial body of law which gives school authorities the right to discipline students for "conduct by the student, in class or out of it, which for

---

[1] "Academic Freedom and Civil Liberties of Students in Colleges and Universities," American Civil Liberties Union, April, 1970.

any reason—whether it stems from time, place, or type of behavior—materially disrupts classwork or involves substantial disorder or invasion of the rights of others. . . ."

This so-called Tinker Case (Tinker v. Des Moines Independent School District, 393, U.S. 503, 512) was a landmark decision in 1969 and any discussion of students and the law has to proceed from that case. In essence, this Supreme Court decision does two things: It establishes that high school students enjoy First Amendment rights, perhaps not to the full extent of adults, but certainly to the extent that the school cannot whimsically or arbitrarily inhibit the free expression of political ideas. It also prohibits the school from infringing on free speech because of an "undifferentiated fear of or apprehension of disturbance." The Tinker case clearly *does* force school administrators to pay far more attention to due process than they had previously. But it by no means renders them incapable of maintaining reasonable discipline, which (so long as the punishment fits the crime) includes expulsion. The language in Tinker is very clear: *"Conduct by a student, in class or out of it, which for any reason—whether it stems from time, place, or type of behavior—materially disrupts classwork or involves substantial disorder or invasion of the rights of others, is not immunized by the constitutional guaranty of freedom of speech."* Tinker *is* the law of the land, at least for the moment, and it may be some time before it is changed. It does *not* bind the hands of university administrators.

There is perhaps a parallel here in the trial of the Chicago Seven, when the court was violently disrupted by the defendants. To those who maintain that courts are rigid and unbending in their view of "due process" and in any explicit or implicit violation of the Bill of Rights and yield not at all in absolutely literal interpretations of the wording, let it be noted that within a few months of the Chicago trial (in Evans v. the United States) the Supreme Court ruled that violent and disruptive defendants do not have the right (Sixth Amendment) to "be confronted with the witnesses against them," but may be removed from the courtroom and tried *in absentia.* This swift decision was unanimous with even that recalcitrant libertarian Justice Douglas going along.

Until a very few years ago, the disciplinary measures which any college or university could employ were determined by the institution's role *in loco parentis;* that is to say, the institution acted and was entitled to act as surrogate parent. Many smaller institutions still serve that role. The multiversity, the huge campus institution, cannot do so, especially with students living both on and off campus.

Under the surrogate parent concept, the students' civil or constitutional rights were no more at issue than they are at issue in the family child-parent relationship. If an institution had a set of rules, if those rules were violated, "let the punishment fit the crime," and that was that.

It is no longer that. The multiversity gives rise to all sorts of new questions. What right has the university, when the student is off campus, to pass on his conduct at all? If university rules and regulations *on* campus, if campus law, so to speak, duplicates community law (town, county, state or federal statutes), does a university have the right to assign punishment beyond that which the community has the responsibility for assigning? Who, in other words, has jurisdiction?

Students, however, *have* increasingly challenged university disciplinary action in court. Yet there is sufficient precedent to lead to the conclusion that the courts will not often assume that there is a cause of action if the infraction is minor and the punishment *does* fit the crime. The trouble arises when the consequences of the alleged misconduct deeply affect the student's future. In long-term suspension or expulsion, the courts have increasingly tended to accept student adversary proceedings as proper and necessary, and to assert that "due process" is required.

It is at this juncture that university administrators grow timorous. *They* are being sued for action they thought imperative. *They* are now involved in cumbersome and very divisive adversary proceedings. *They* are now subject to further student strikes and violence in the name of the "martyred" ones. Indeed, in light of these consequences, the violent ones invite expulsion precisely because the ensuing court action is fuel for further turmoil on campus. Thus the violent one not only uses the freedom he has on campus to attack that freedom, he further uses the court (the basic purpose of which is to protect individual rights) to destroy individual rights.

It simply cannot be said that today's student, whose mean age is slightly over twenty-one years, is a non-person as regards due process and civil and constitutional rights. But it simply must be said that the courts must: (1) act with dispatch in such cases; (2) examine critically whether indeed they are not being cynically used; and (3) determine by *very* critical examination whether indeed in the case of a given expulsion, due process *is* involved.

Point number three above should probably be number one because the simple fact is that precedent which would require a court to accept, in the name of due process, all causes of action as legitimate simply because a student's lawyer says so, simply does not exist. Indeed, one of the prominent author-

ities on the subject, William W. Van Alstyne, Professor of
Law at Duke University (himself a strong defender of student
rights), says: "The federal cases involving procedural due
process for students have been disposed of by courts below
the level of the United States Supreme Court [the Tinker
Case had not yet been decided] and thus their utterances
on this subject are not necessarily the last word. *Indeed, a
number of Federal courts disagree among themselves respect-
ing the requisite degree of college due process* [italics mine]."[2]

But let us assume that in a given case of expulsion the
court does examine the allegations critically, is aware of the
probable campus consequences and still feels that due process
and a trial is necessary in the name of fairness and the individual's protection. So be it. The university has not lost its
power to expel and by *prior* preparation and with good legal
advice can expedite the process, reduce the violent one's
power of disruption, and greatly enhance its chances of
winning its case.

To do this it must: (1) not use expulsion whimsically; (2)
have published and widely disseminated its rules with great
emphasis on specificity, that is, the language must not be
vague and generalized; (3) be prepared to charge the student
with a specific infraction of a specific rule in writing at least
ten days before it provides for a hearing at which (4) the
student is permitted to inspect the evidence, allegations, ex-
hibits or affidavits pertaining to his case; (5) the student
should be informed of his right to have counsel at the hearing;
(6) the student or his counsel may question any witness at
the hearing; (7) the results should be written up fully and
presented to the student for his perusal.

If such procedures are extant, if such rules are set forth,

<hr>

[2] See *Protest, op. cit.,* p. 539.

if such a hearing is held, there is a very good chance that the matter will not get to court at all, and an excellent chance that if it does get to court, the trial will be shorter and the chances of victory better and the chance of violence lessened.

What could happen, indeed, what I think *has* happened, based on countless conversations with university administrators and many letters from them, is that they feel that the greatest single power they have, ultimately, to maintain order on their campuses, the power to expel, has been seriously curtailed and diminished by the courts.

No one can accuse the American Civil Liberties Union of right-wing tendencies or of a conservative view of students' rights. In its latest pamphlet addressed to students, however, it warns: "Actions which deprive others of the right to speak or be heard, involve taking over buildings that disrupt the educational process, incarceration of or assaults on persons, destruction of property and rifling of files, are anti-civil libertarian and incompatible with the nature and functions of educational institutions."[3]

And, considering the source, two more brief quotes: "Demonstrators, however, have no right to deprive others of the opportunity to speak or be heard; take hostages, physically obstruct the movement of others; or otherwise disrupt the educational or institutional processes in a way that interferes with the safety or freedom of others."[4] And, "Students, like teachers, have a right to identify themselves as members of a particular academic community. But they also have the moral obligation not to misrepresent the views of others in their academic community."[5]

So the university administrator is often not as paralyzed

---

[3] Report of April, 1970, p. 7.
[4] *Ibid.,* p. 17.
[5] *Ibid.*

as he seems to feel. Indeed, one prestigious lawyer who wrote me (his "avocation" is students and the law) said, "He [the university president] is certainly not unique in this position. This same uncertainty faces our clients (and their counsel) in antitrust, unfair competition, libel and hundreds of other areas. . . . The general public and the overwhelming number of judges are fed up with student insolence, to say nothing of violence and destruction. What the judges want is a well-documented case, effectively presented. The law is there." And he concluded, "I am not persuaded . . . that law and order and reasonable discipline is no longer attainable under existing court decisions. This simply is not true."

The university administrator seems often to overlook another legal aspect of the matter. The university need not always assume a defensive stance. Given any number of circumstances, it can take the offense. It is no more unreasonable (nor, given the body of law on the subject, should it be considered unusual) for the university to sue the student. Why not?

For instance, there is nothing in the law that prevents a university from obtaining a restraining order. A restraining order can be issued *ex parte* (i.e., the student is not a party to it), and quickly, if the administrator can give sufficient evidence that, unrestrained, a genuine danger to the institution exists. The university would not, of course, seek to restrain thousands of students, but, with trouble brewing, it could have the court issue such orders to the known troublemakers—the few hard-core organizers. Can many university administrators today say that they simply do not know who the real militants—on and off campus—are? I suspect that they cannot. They may not know them all. They know many of them.

A restraining order is, of course, temporary. Within a few

days, or a week, the university would have to appear in court to "show cause." At that time a permanent injunction might be issued or the restraining order might be lifted—depending on the evidence. The point is, that with trouble brewing (an anti-war rally scheduled on campus, and anti-ROTC rally on campus, an anti-Dow Chemical or military recruiter rally—accompanied by rumors and threats of bombings and burnings), those "few days" of the restraining order could very well be critical in preventing the "spark plugs" or the "fuse lighters" from converting a rally into a riot.

Even, indeed, when a building *has* been occupied and classes *are* being disrupted, the university administrator has a legal weapon which he can employ *short* of calling for the police. Knowing that the appearance of the police or other anti-riot forces on campus may quickly polarize things and lead to riot, he can enjoin the students occupying the building. Again, he cannot enjoin thousands, or even hundreds of students. He must know the hard core, and they must be named in the injunction.

Contrary to what is apparently a widespread misunderstanding of the injunctive process among university administrators, there is very great latitude in what the courts permit. For example, an ROTC building is now being occupied (the case is an actual one). Initially some 100 students enter. The academic vice president enters and informs them that they are in violation of university rules. They reply that they want the ROTC building closed to all persons and ROTC personnel for the duration of the strike (three days). The vice president asks them to leave. All but about 40 leave. Among the 40 were perhaps 10 "hard core," the names well known to the administration.

The administration now has the choice: Close the building

or enjoin the known agitators. But an injunction conjures
up a vision of police and arrests on the spot—and that in
the midst of a tense campus situation and while a rally with
several thousand students (thus far peaceful) is being conducted on campus. The administration chooses to close the
ROTC building.

In this instance, the peace was kept and that was salutary.
Whether in the long run the action was wise remains to be
seen. One point is, however, that the injunctive process need
not have involved the police at all and thus need not have
led to confrontation.

A deputy sheriff in civilian clothing and unarmed could
merely have entered the building (the doors were open) and
served the papers. The injunction could simply have said,
in effect, that unless this building is vacated in (one hour,
two hours, "any" hours), you are in contempt of court. At
the appointed hour, the sheriff would return and give them
notice that they have (five minutes, ten minutes, "any"
minutes) to vacate. If they refused, he would simply go his
way. At any time thereafter (a day, a week, ten days), the
individual students could be individually served for contempt.

Riots are short-lived; hot emotions cool quickly. The arrests
could have been made in the quiet aftermath, individually.
For what purpose then? Because the "hard core" would not
then have won hands down. Because "the next time" there
might well be second thoughts. Because the administration
could not then so readily be accused of having "capitulated,"
it could defend itself to regents, legislators and angry citizens
as *not* having yielded. It had neither under- nor over-reacted.
There is much to recommend that posture.

The larger point is that court "permissiveness," the court's
"new" emphasis on due process and student rights, have not

strait-jacketed university administrators. They have many legal recourses and many routes to take, provided that they are alert and have good legal counsel. Laws and processes do not constitute the answer to campus unrest, nor, probably, can they prevent all campus violence, however well handled. But the law and courts, properly employed, can be of enormous help in the crisis of the American university today. And the university needs all the help it can get.

Behind the question of students and the law, however, lies a larger question. No one who has consistently read anything about riots and the police can avoid some exceedingly troublesome questions, often responded to with some exceedingly dubious answers. Quite obviously, it is to the militant students' great advantage to respond to any police action with the loud cry of "police brutality." Just as obviously, however, there *has* been police brutality. Thoroughly documented cases of innocent, adult persons mistakenly caught in student off- (and on-) campus riots, are chilling evidence that "police brutality" has occurred with distressing frequency. *Look, Life* and other magazines have run carefully researched articles and personal testimonials on the subject, and reliable, trained reporters and television personnel have far too often themselves been the victims not merely of extralegal procedures, but of brutal and illegal incarceration. If respect for law and order is to be restored in America (and it must be), it cannot be done by sticking "Support Your Local Police" decals on automobile bumpers and it cannot be done by issuing American flags for police to wear on their uniforms. The police themselves can help restore their image—but they will need help in turn.

The question, Do the police and police courts dispense equal justice, must all too often be answered in the negative.

Any lawyer who has spent any time in a big-city criminal court can vouch for that. And still another specter stands behind police forces which have too often lost their cool. What must be the reaction, say, of a policeman in New York City who knows that for a serious crime the odds are 200 to 1 that the man will never go to prison on the charge? What does the policeman in Washington, D.C., think, knowing that the average delay between his arresting a man on a felony charge and the actual trial is ten months? What does the Los Angeles policeman do when he knows that the court's case load is growing ten times faster than the population? What goes through the mind of a policeman in Dallas when he sees that a defense attorney has written for *Life* magazine: "Delay is my best weapon. Time will beat any case if you have enough of it."

In short, the criminal courts in urban America are failing miserably and the further fact is that this failure greatly damages the innocent and greatly benefits the guilty, and the still further fact is that the greatest damage is done to the under-privileged and dispossessed, the blacks, Chicanos and Puerto Ricans—along with the poor whites. And what of the honest policeman, the policeman who believes in equal justice under the law? It either corrupts him or renders him frustrated and cynical, which, in itself, is a kind of corruption.

Chief Justice Warren Burger gives clear warning: "Many people, though not all, will be deterred from serious crimes if they believe that justice is swift and sure. *Today no one thinks that it is* [italics mine]."

And that includes college students. It very surely includes college students and it is part and parcel of their attitude toward police, especially when they appear on campus. The police represent, and in very concrete form, the morass of inequities that stand behind them.

Short of very extensive legal and court reform (which even the conservative Chief Justice recognizes as imperative in an August 7, 1970, issue of *Life* magazine), there will remain among a very large number of students an abiding mistrust of police forces—and that mistrust will quickly turn to violence, even among moderate students, when police appear on campuses.

Many of my generation exhibited shock and dismay when Yale University exploded over the case of Black Panther Bobby Seale. They did not, I think, understand that behind that explosion lay the larger mistrust of the American system of justice as it operates with regard to the disadvantaged in the lower courts. And perhaps they did not understand another fact which troubles a great many students deeply. My generation abhors the Black Panthers. The Panthers stand for everything that is violent, criminal and reprehensible. But there are very few students who have not read Panther Eldridge Cleaver's *Soul on Ice,* and there are very few who do not believe that the police have, in fact, conducted a vendetta against the Panthers.

There have been no definitive studies of the Panthers. There have been no comprehensive investigations into the charges which blacks and whites alike have made against the police. What evidence *is* available seems to sustain the Panther argument that they have, in fact, often acted in self-defense.

So "student problems and the law" cannot be viewed simply in the context of restraining orders, injunctions, due process and the powers of the university administration. The problems are deeper and more complex than that. They reach down to the root of the matter. What is wrong with the judicial system at the lower level—the level where the poor, the indigent, the disadvantaged meet it?

With few exceptions, including students, Americans have high regard for the federal judiciary, the circuit courts and the Supreme Court. With few exceptions they admire the high principles which emerged from English common law and evolved to American legal principles. But with increasing vehemence, and most especially among the young, Americans are evincing contempt and even abhorrence for the criminal courts and the lower courts in general. And that is a very dangerous thing, for it is precisely there that the average American meets the law. What is the answer?

Chief Justice Burger says: ". . . there is a remedy . . . the people have the right and the ultimate power to change the system. Neither the laws nor the Constitution are too sacred to change and the decisions of judges are not holy writ. . . . We should not hesitate to make basic changes or discard mechanisms which do not work to the benefit of society."

Well, then, says the student—and well, then, say I, we had better go about this pretty fast. Because the mechanisms on that level are not working. And, once again, it is late, very late.

Chapter 7

The Historian and the Crystal Ball

WHAT was once called the "dysmal science," economics, has risen so rapidly and so far in public esteem that today it might better be called the "miraculous science." No government could function without its battery of economists, no bank can feel secure without a consulting economist. News magazines employ their own economists—and it is a rare department of economics on any campus whose faculty is not off consulting with some company or other part of the time.

It is a little puzzling, though, that historians have remained so academic and so rarely engage in "projections." They have been notably reluctant in the past even to make comments on the current scene in the light of the past.

This is strange since it is fairly obvious that cause and effect do operate in the affairs of mankind and that there is a cyclical nature to events and that the past *does* throw light on the present. Moreover, one would think that there is no inherent reason for the historian's crystal ball to be murkier than the economist's.

In the past year or two, however, historians *have* begun

to peep out of the classroom to comment on the current scene and even, in a few cases, to make predictions. If the economists are any indication of the way these things go, it should surprise no one that historians don't agree with each other. The trouble is that events don't speak for themselves but only as historians interpret them, and given identical raw material, historians are perfectly capable of coming to opposite conclusions.

Newsweek magazine decided to chance it anyway, and in its July 6, 1970 issue asked six of America's most prestigious historians to comment on the "American Crisis." *Look* magazine on July 14 ran a long, ominous essay by Henry Steele Commager entitled "Is Freedom Dying in America?" And if one wishes to compound the confusion, one can go back a year or two in the *Saturday Review, Atlantic* and *Harper's* and find a few other historians getting into the act.

Newsweek's issue was stimulating because the choice of historians guaranteed disagreement. The late Richard Hofstadter of Columbia was an enormously prolific and respected historian for twenty years. He was a liberal, or as he put it "a 30's-vintage 'radical liberal.'" Cornell's Andrew Hacker is a Republican and a "conservative"; Eugene D. Genovese of the University of Rochester is a Marxist; Staughton Lynd is a "New Left" historian; Daniel J. Boorstin is Director of the Smithsonian Institution and a moderate; Arthur M. Schlesinger, Jr., of the City University of New York, is a Democrat and a "liberal."

These gentlemen all agree that there is unusual trouble abroad in the land. They do not agree on its origins; they do not agree on its extent; they do not agree on solutions.

So why bother? Because several of them have some pithy things to say about the younger generation—and the older.

And because what they have to say bears on what I want to say about the younger generation and its ignorance of history. I am not interpreting what these historians are saying; I am simply abstracting phrases.

Peering into the gloom, Hofstadter remarked: "Radicalism is irresistibly chic. . . . I don't think the young people now are going to have their minds changed very much by arguments. They have to be profoundly surprised by something before they will begin to reconsider their experience. . . . The kids dislike the idea that they are thinking and acting as an elite, but they are."

Asked if he thought there was an "authentic revolutionary feeling involved," Hacker replied that he did not. He said, "The talk is awfully loose" and said that today's radical young simply wanted "to do something right away. But the consistent work, the study, the application, the risk-taking that goes into the making of a Lenin or a Rosa Luxemburg or any number of other classic revolutionary figures don't seem to me to be present among many of them. What you have in place of revolutionaries are clowns like Abbie Hoffman and Jerry Rubin."

Eugene D. Genovese quite predictably blames the whole trouble on the failure of "our vaunted capitalist social system," and says that "young people, who have little or no investment of their own lives in the material conditions on which they have been raised, are psychologically in much better condition to take a hard and sometimes brutal view of the qualities of life their parents' struggle has purchased." Their elders, says Genovese, because of their "investment" respond with "fear and confusion."

A cool Daniel J. Boorstin, who takes the calmest view of them all, says that America is suffering from "a case of hypo-

chondria," and says, "Unless we begin to believe that we won't
be dead until morning, we may not be up to the daily tasks
of a healthy life." "In a word," says Boorstin, "we have lost
our sense of history." Boorstin goes on to deal at some length
with the utter necessity of having to know where you have
been in order to know where you are and remarks, "The
best antidote, then, against ruthless, absolute and simple-
minded utopias has been American history itself . . . for
we have wandered out of history. And all in the name of
virtue and social conscience . . . we are all overwhelmed
by the instant moment." And Boorstin adds, "Unless we give
up the voguish reverence for youth and for the 'culturally
deprived,' unless we cease to look to the vulgar community
as the arbiters of our schools, of our art and our literature,
and of all our culture, we will never have the will to de-
provincialize our minds."

Though none of the six historians involved agree on many
essentials, there is a strange commonality even in their approach to disagreement. They may be wary of analogies; they
all nevertheless exhibit a belief in a certain cyclicalism, and
all agree that there are some very old ingredients in today's
combustible mixture of problems. But, as Arthur Schlesinger,
Jr. puts it: "Is the contemporary crisis more profound than
other crises in our history? This seems to me an unanswerable
question, because a crisis surmounted always seems less terrible than a crisis in being."

None of the six would deny, however, that America has
faced profoundly serious crises in the past. None, I am sure,
would deny that there is a profound lot to be learned from
the study of these crises—and serious consequences for a
country that loses an essential sense of its history. Genovese
says that the young see our present problems more clearly

than we do because "they have little or no investment of their own lives in the material conditions on which they have been raised." I, with Boorstin, would say that they do *not,* precisely because they know too little of their past.

One could dwell at length on why this state of affairs exists, but the nub of it is this: We don't teach history any more—and that is my generation's fault. We teach world civics or social studies in the grades and high schools. We emphasize "nowness" and we emphasize our ills. The study of history as history is hard and sometimes tedious. Most learning involves pain and tedium, educationists' theories to the contrary notwithstanding. So we sugarcoat it—or we simply don't teach it.

It is not that good teachers don't exist or that the average teacher is lazy. It is simply that our elementary and secondary school system is shot through—and has been for some years—with infectious "nowness" and with the idea that if pain, tedium or sweat enter into the learning process, something is wrong with the process. The educationists have many pedagogical formulae to make learning an unmitigated joy, but in fact what they do is simply to dump in more sugar. No discipline of the mind, no hard and tedious hours of reading—just more sugar.

If the younger generation knew a modicum of American history they would, for instance, regardless of how the events have been variously interpreted by historians, know that again and again and over again, America has been confronted with deep social, economic, and moral crises. They would know that the American people have been repeatedly and deeply divided over very basic issues. One could not even make a simple catalog of these issues without extending a chapter to a thick volume.

There is tremendous emphasis today on the disadvantaged
and the dispossessed in our society. We are acutely conscious
of the plight of the migrant worker, of Appalachia, of poverty
where poverty should not and must not exist.

Yet at one time, just for instance, the *whole* of the laboring
"class" in America was disadvantaged and dispossessed. They
existed only by the sufferance of the employer. They had no
"rights"—no right to strike, no right to bargain collectively.
It was the duty of government, under the prevailing economic
theory, to aid business but not labor. President Eliot of
Harvard could assert that the closed shop was un-American.
Others believed it to be treason. Capital was beautifully and
thoroughly organized and backed by government. Labor was
utterly unorganized, exploited and demoralized. The courts
saw no merit in labor organizations nor did they in any way
recognize labor's right to a decent standard of living, a maximum hour workday, elementary health and living standards.
This did not involve a few hundred thousand people; it involved millions.

The *majority* of Americans had thus been bludgeoned by
the industrial revolution subsequent to 1865 into a state of
poverty, tenantry and, as Morison and Commager put it in
their two-volume history of America, there existed "monstrous
perversions in the employment of women and children and
in the treatment of the aged, the incompetent and the infirm."

The point to be noted is that between the farmer and the
laborer, *most* of America's citizenry suffered want, deprivation
of the severest kind—and this in a "fabulously rich" economic
environment. In this land of abundance and plenty, there was
never enough food, clothing or shelter for millions upon millions of people.

There is simply no comparison between *relative* poverty

then and now. The problems which faced reformers then were overwhelmingly greater in magnitude, both in terms of the number of people involved and in terms of the depths of their deprivation, than the problems of poverty and deprivation today. Moreover, there had been an almost total breakdown in political integrity; the cities were hell holes of graft and vice, the entire American administrative system was encrusted with red tape, inefficiency and dishonesty.

And moreover, as reformers began to pull America back from the brink of awesome catastrophe, they faced not only poverty amid plenty, but a spiritual and ethical crisis of great magnitude. The manufacture of impure foods, dangerous drugs, infected milk, the total lack of safety regulations in industrial plants and mines, the utter disregard for basic humanitarianism by corporations and government, had led not merely to simmering anger and suppressed fury—it had led to an awesome malaise among the victims themselves.

Now these are simply facts, readily converted into appalling statistics. The battle for reform and rebirth took place on various fronts between, say, 1890 and 1930. Out of the battle (which often spilled over into violence), a battle which was always hard and bitter, there arose reform of profound extent—reform which changed moral and ethical standards, reform which cast government in an entirely new role, reform which changed, and basically, the way one American looked at another, reform which changed almost all American economic and political philosophy and profoundly altered political and economic structures and institutions.

In this drive for reform there were setbacks, failures and plateaus. There were false prophets and extremists to be carried along as heavy albatrosses around the necks of those who knew that the hope lay in reform rather than revolution—and who knew that victory lay in persistence, hard and continual work, careful planning, pragmatic ends and more work and organization and dedication. And the simple fact is this: They won. They did not create Utopia; they did not solve all problems; they did not bring joy and enlightenment to all Americans. But they won. They altered America forever; they changed something which went to the near edge of human nature.

The "New Left" historians and the Marxists would disagree that the crisis then was as deep as it is now. I would simply say that it was deeper. Far more Americans suffered then and suffered more from their ills, per capita, than suffer now. I would submit that "reform" then faced vastly greater odds (in the form of the "establishment") than it faces today. I would submit that the "malaise" (a word the despairers fondly embrace today) was greater then than it is now. And I would submit that reformers then had far fewer tools and far fewer channels through which to work than have reformers today.

But, says today's youthful zealot, that took *years* to accomplish. I can only say that it did, indeed—and every year was worth it, that every year was an enormous investment in a future so much better for the next generation of *average* Americans (and the next and the next) that the bright legacy of that effort ran far into the country's future.

Why can't it be done again? It can. And faster and farther. The tools are sharper, the precedents exist in abundance. One builds on past progress and there has been vast progress. Again, if the confused and despairing young American would read some history—just straight textbook stuff, if nothing else—he would see that he is not just "now," not confronted with overwhelming "newness," not isolated from the past, not cut off from the future and, above all (in the light of myriad examples in his country's past), not "helpless."

But, they say, there is this terrible war. They say there is no precedent for that and no precedent for the way they feel about it. It *is* a terrible war. But it *will* end and be careful about the precedent argument.

Vietnam, presumably the longest war in our history (it is not) and presumably the only guerrilla war we have fought (it is not), and presumably the most expensive per enemy killed (it is not) has admittedly been, and is, a terribly divisive event on the present American scene.

Our longest war, of course, was our war with the American Indian—which, in a strictly military sense, we lost. In 1868, President Grant, considering this endless series of engagements, considering the predictions of total victory which had been floating around for many years, asked for a report on the state of the war. The report was made in due course by the Commissioner of Indian Affairs. The Commissioner wrote:

> It would seem that the cost price of Indians slain in the Florida War, in the Sioux War (1852–1854) and the late Cheyenne War, has been on a fair average about a million dollars each, and if our Indian troubles are to be ended by exterminating the race, it is evident, at the present rate of one Indian killed per month, that achievement will be completed at the end of exactly 25,000 years; and if each dead Indian is to cost the same hereafter as heretofore, the precise sum total we will have to expend is 300 billion. . . . But besides the cost to the treasury, it is found by actual comparison . . . that the slaying of every Indian costs us the lives of 25 whites, so that the extermination process must bring about the slaughter of 7,500,000 of our people.

In the end, of course, the Indian capitulated not because we ever beat him on the field (indeed, he far more often beat us) but because we killed 85,000,000 buffalo, the staple of Indian life, the core of his economy, and because we weakened him with smallpox and whiskey.

And the Indian War (that series of clashes which lasted from the early eighteenth century nearly to the twentieth) was very divisive. A substantial and vocal number of Americans deplored it over a very long period of time as immoral, improper, inhuman and wasteful.

Now, indeed, one cannot equate that war with the Vietnam War in terms of its effect on the American populace or in terms of the economy. But one should not stop there. Let the young "now" generation consider the *violent* divisiveness of the Civil War. What is more divisive than 600,000 dead and wounded Americans? Moreover, it was a war deplored by hundreds of thousands of Americans during its course. Let the present draft resisters read of the magnitude of the draft riots of 1863; let the young "this-is-brand-new" generation study the violent American opposition to the Mexican War, to the Spanish-American War and to World War I. The latter brought forth opposition which was extraordinarily widespread and often violent.

It is not my purpose to review our wars in order of magnitude and resistance. It is merely to assert that moral indignation over war is not the sole property of the younger generation. It's not my assertion that analogies are particularly striking in this respect. I merely suggest that they exist and that it would behoove many of the young to study them.

Crisis on the right? John Birchers, Minute Men? The extreme right has always been with us. Look to the period during and after World War I. No right wing movement of today can compare to the right wing as embodied in the Federal Sedition Act of 1918 which was at least as repressive as the Alien and Sedition Act of 1798. No suppressive measures even suggested by today's right wing can compare to the actuality of suppression in the 1920's—the great "Red Scare." Massive repressive measures in blatant and open violation of the constitutional rights of Americans were passed in state after state, to say nothing of the Federal Government.

Racism? The Ku Klux Klan was enormously powerful politically in both South and North. There was deep-seated anti-Semitism running through those years as well.

Yet mark this well, this powerful, hate-ridden, fear-clothed, nativist, fundamentalist orgy was over by 1925. We survived it; we took a long look and stopped it—there wasn't even enough power left in this viciously ominous black cloud of 1922 to stop the nomination of Al Smith in 1928.

There was a recrudescence of this in the McCarthy era—a pale shadow but a shadow—and a disgraceful one. And we stopped it. Again, as a hundred times before, the pendulum swung. So you say America can't change, won't change, that the country is now what it always will be?

But you could only say that if you knew nothing of its past. The pendulum swings, but it is terribly important to observe that it does not swing by itself. It is pushed. In America, like a true pendulum, it has a tendency for the center. With no one pushing it at all (which will never happen), it would simply find dead center and stay there. But however and irrespective of who is pushing, the American pendulum is always attracted to the center. That is not true of all countries; it *is* true of America.

Yet there is no guarantee at all that, left or right, it will not swing too far. It did in 1860; it came close in 1933.

It is now, today, rightward bound. It has very considerable momentum—how much, none of us knows. But this much, at least, we can assert with considerable accuracy. How far it swings to the right depends in large part on how hard and in what ways it is pushed from the left.

If the nature of this thrust is strong dissent within the patterns designed for and already deeply woven into the fabric of the structures of government and society, the move to the right will slacken in pace and there will emerge an era of new economic, social and political priorities and a reordering of life styles—in short, an era of deep-reaching reform. If the thrust from the left lies in the acceptance of violence as a means to an end, if it is inchoate and unordered and relies for its substance on myth, ignorant rhetoric and the substitution of gut for brain, the result can only be suppression. The pendulum will swing beyond its capacity to return. Hard, cold and implacable, the extreme right will have its way.

It is fashionable now for the young militant to cite but one historical analogy. It is, apparently, the only one he has. National Socialism came to Germany because Hitler cried "order" when students and dissenters disrupted order. That, says the young militant, is what is happening in America today. The call for law and order, the emphasis placed upon it by "the right," is Hitlerian. We are today where Germany was in 1933. How too bad, if they are going to appeal to history at all, that they appeal so inanely. Even in the most superficial sense the analogy is false.

Consider very carefully this thought, reading the words without distorting their simple meaning: As between order and justice, remember that without order there can be no justice at all.

Chapter 8

The Faculty

MAYBE the place to begin with what disturbs me about my own generation is at home—for me, a faculty. I joined a faculty late in life, as academic matters go. When I got my Ph.D. in 1951, I decided not to teach. Jobs were hard to get then, but there was a far more basic reason. I had had enough of the closed-in unreality of academia. Periodically, throughout the long graduate grind, I would listen to a professor expound (not only in history, but in other disciplines) and I would think, "Sir, you can't be for real."

I had just come from four fairly real years of World War II, two of them overseas, and I found the difference between the world as I saw it and as "the faculty" saw it too variant to want to be part of a faculty. So I went off and did many things, and it was fifteen years before I joined a faculty. I did so then because I felt sure that I had changed and that, surely, they had, too.

Maybe, indeed, neither I nor "faculties" had changed at all, or maybe we had both changed greatly, but one thing remained. I found then, five years ago, and I find now, that "faculties" are still isolated, insulated and removed. That, of course, is an unconscionable generalization. There are on any campus dozens and even hundreds of exceptions. But I will stick with the assertion. Not only are they removed from "the community" in which they live and in a very essential respect from the larger community of the nation and the world, but they are removed from students—and herein lies a critical problem which the student recognizes clearly and "the professor" does not.

I think perhaps faculties could survive intact in isolation from the everyday affairs of the community, large and small (because of the unique nature of their training and work), but I do *not* think they can survive intact in their present forms in "intra" isolation from the students.

The name of the game is the student—undergraduate or graduate. Universities do not exist for faculties; they exist for students. And, the larger the university, the thicker the barrier between student and teacher. Research is a vital aspect of academic life because good teaching is ultimately rooted in it. But the researching professor far, far too often is conducting his research for reasons which have nothing to do with students at all. Yet the research is being conducted at their expense. He does not keep adequate office hours, if, indeed, he keeps them at all. When he does, his relationship (particularly on the undergraduate level) with the student is perfunctory, often marked by impatience mixed with arrogance. The fact that the student may have waited a week or two for his "appointment," the fact that he may have had to chase the professor all over campus for two days simply to get a card signed, makes no difference to the professor at all.

A professor does research for any number of reasons. Very

high on the list, however, is that if he publishes, he is promoted; if he doesn't, he isn't. And this is not confined to schools with an avowed "publish or perish" system. It is widespread enough to be termed a common practice.

Also high on the list is that as "consultants" professors are often very well paid, whether their research is on or off campus. So it is simply a matter of money. Money or no, the real expense involved is for the student. He does not get what he paid for.

Fairly high on the list is the fact that a relatively large number of professors simply don't like to teach, but they do like to research. In that scheme of things, the student is simply a means to an end and an annoyance at that.

Whatever the reasons, part of the cause of the simmering resentment on many campuses is caused by the insulation and isolation of the faculty. And of the faculty members of any institution, the tenured full professor is the most guilty. So the students turn to younger faculty members (who have themselves just survived the system and deeply resent it) for aid and comfort. Acting together, they begin to raise hell— justified and necessary hell because there *are* so few other ways to change the system. It is, indeed, via this route that the young, frustrated faculty get themselves stereotyped as "firebrands." It's via this route (identification with and sympathy for the students) that they sometimes *become* firebrands. This, also, is one of the reasons that dissent, which turns into violence, is much more prevalent on large campuses than on small.

It is my own experience that students badly want and badly need intimate contact with their professors aside from the lecture platform or the seminar table. They want *and are entitled to* close contact with the professor, and alone with him, when they feel the need for it. Granted that this is difficult at huge schools, even there, an awareness on the part of the faculty (an awareness uncommon at any of them with which I am familiar) that the student has priority, that the student comes first, could defuse a substantial amount of volatile discontent. But I see no indication that this is changing. The student sees no indication that it is changing either. His anger and frustration are thoroughly understandable. He is being cheated, day by day, and he knows it.

Tightly sealed in, plethorically self-satisfied, his ego fed by a sort of mutual admiration society (his colleagues), his mind set on the structure as it is, his myopia increasing concerning the students, the tenured full professor goes his own remarkably free and self-centered way—and then wonders why the student is resentful. He has come to believe, in his isolation, that the *faculty* is the university; he fights for *faculty* prerogatives, for his *department's* welfare. He asserts himself, in other words, for *his* needs, *his* welfare, *his* place on the totem pole, *his* influence in the faculty senate. But how about the student?

I have said before that the curricula at most American universities have changed drastically over the past decade in the face of need. Faculty attitudes toward students have not. And it is not sufficient merely to change the curriculum, because the key to whether the change works or not is in the hands of the faculty.

Nor is the student's legitimate complaint on campus limited to discontent with the performance of the faculty. He has every right to resent being the integer he has become.

One of my students came to me last year in a state of barely contained fury. As at most schools, our grading system is computerized, and this student, whose grade point average was very high, had received a C in Piano. It was not the C that bothered him; it was the fact that he had never enrolled in a course in Piano. It was not the fact that the computer had made a mistake that bothered him; it was rather that when he went to the registrar's office to have the mistake corrected, the person at the window insisted that my student *had* taken Piano and *had* gotten a C. After convincing the registrars office he had not taken Piano, the student spent hours carrying petitions and forms and cards around the campus to get the C in Piano off his transcript and grade report. He had, he calculated, spent seven hours, in all, getting the correction made. "What this goddam place needs," he said, "is an Ombudsman who can cut through this unholy maze of rules, forms, machinery and foolishness so that we can tend to the business of going to school." And this at an institution of only 8,000 students!

It may be true that the American university is no more overstructured than a corporation of commensurate size and it probably *is* true that it is less bureaucraticized than most arms of government—local, state and national. The point is that a university is *not* a corporation or a government bureau, and the more critical point is that a student is *not* an employee. He is not a means, he is an end; he is not a cog, he is the wheel. To stamp him, index him, card him and spindle him is not the *raison d'être* for the university's existence. Yet often, very, very often, the student is the means to some other end, and he knows it.

Whether the ultimate answer is to break the huge institutions down into many small ones, or whether that answer lies more in a change of faculty and administrative attitude— and a *pronounced* change, I cannot say. But Vietnam War or no Vietnam War, the student, increasingly dissatisfied with what he is getting in the name of education, will continue to cause substantial trouble until changes are made.

It could be that the new, young faculty, faculty now in their twenties, could bring about this change, but I do not believe we can wait that long.

The so-called "free university" movement both on and off hundreds of American campuses today indicates that the hour is late. It will not do to write this movement off. Granted, as I have previously, that many changes and reforms proposed all over the country by proponents of the "free university" are utterly foolish, the movement itself represents a deep and, I believe, an abiding frustration and dissatisfaction with the higher educational process in America. Debate the issue as I will (and have) with hundreds of students from Boston to Los Angeles, I cannot escape the ultimate conviction that they are right. I cannot escape their logic nor their earnestness. I cannot pit the younger generation against the older in this vitally important area and come to any conclusion other than that they are right and we are wrong.

Part and parcel of student dissatisfaction with the university today extends beyond the faculty and the bureaucracy to the structure itself. They object to the departmentalization and compartmentalization of learning. Most of them do not know that the objection is a very old one, and fewer still know that experimental schools ranging from St. John's to Antioch and from Reed to Vera Cruz have tackled the problem head-on. The fact remains that the compartmentalization is really untouched—and, once again, the students are right.

University faculties and administrators (mostly the former) have a favorite bit of jargon all their own. The key word is "interdisciplinary." I would hazard a guess that in the past twenty years, practically every American university or college has either established some kind of "interdisciplinary" program, or has a bundle of plans in its files. The hard fact remains that few of these programs work. The fact that you have a system which gives a student a little math, a little history, a little science and a little literature, a little music and a little physics and that you mix all this up with a little lab work and a little field work and a little philosophy and a little pottery and a little sociology doesn't solve a basic problem. Neither does the fact that you place one umbrella over the process, give it a special name, a director with an office, and describe its wonders in a catalog.

There still sits the department of history with an enormous vested interest in continuing to do precisely what it is doing, only more of it, and determinedly defending the *distinctness* of history from philosophy, from economics, from anthropology, from computer science, from ecology, and from other disciplines. And every other department does likewise—the sciences as well as the non-sciences.

The problem *is not simple* precisely because its roots run deeper than mere vested interest. In an age of specialists, you produce specialists. There are simply very few scholars around with an intellectual background of sufficient breadth to relate with any precision the inextricable connection between specialties. There was a time, of course, when a true scholar was as well versed in philosophy and literature as he was in calculus and Greek. But that day is gone.

No institution, whatever its plan, however experimental, given four short years and given the extent of the sum total of human knowledge can impart to the student the abiding, immutable interconnection and interdependence of that knowledge.

But most assuredly, swift progress could be made not in

abolishing departmental compartmentalization, not in eradi-
cating the parochialism of the specialties, but in substituting
diaphanous membranes rather than brick walls as the substance that isolates one discipline from another.

Pass-fail grades rather than standard grading systems could
easily be instituted for non-majors. And it *would* be feasible
to appoint an Ombudsman with sufficient power not merely
to raise hell with the clanking inefficiency of university
machinery, but also to bend and even break the rigid rules
with which departments seek to exclusivize themselves.

Most universities have a vice president for student affairs
or a dean of students, but these offices are almost invariably
filled by faculty-oriented people. I am simply proposing that
such an officer be militantly a student partisan and that he
be endowed not merely with extraordinary power to bend
and break rules and cut across existing lines, but that he be
given a solid budget and plenty of help.

However, in the last analysis, it is faculty attitude that matters. Devices, new structures, new officers cannot really
change that. Once again, it is late, very late. Let the tenured
full professor take a long look at himself and his students,
his office hours, his research and think very hard about his
own schedule and priorities. Unless he comes to see that the
student stands first in the order of things—that the student
is what it is all about—there is very little chance that unrest
on the campus will abate. And that unrest, mixed with other
student concerns and issues, will make the university campus
a volatile and unpleasant place for a long time to come.

A straight, short-haired, pleasant and slightly frightened
young man goes off to college with a handshake from a proud
father and a kiss from a tearful mother. It is costing a lot
to send him. He is to tend to business and return with an

"education"! He's to hit the books and listen to his professors. The latter have the knowledge. He is to garner it from them. He is to equip himself for the world. Neither his father nor his mother ever had that opportunity. Now the great door is open to the son. The "education" will help him enormously in the future. He will be equipped for living a life, a real life, his mother and father were not equipped for.

Somewhere along the line, a year or two later, the son comes home. His hair is down to his shoulders; he wears beads; his language is strange; he is critical not only of the school, but of his country and the world. He argues with his parents about the process of education, about the state of the world. A quick alienation sets in. Thinks the father, "My God, I have a hippie for a son. They have done that to him at the school. The goddam kid doesn't understand the value of an education." And the son thinks, "I can't get through to them; I can't explain the university. I can't explain the frustrations and hypocrisies. Certainly I have learned something, but it isn't what they wanted me to learn."

Part of what he learned is that he couldn't "garner" much from his professors. He rarely saw them except over the heads of 350 other students. Part of what he heard them say didn't ring true—it rang far off in some chamber removed from the reality he saw around him. It was not false, it was simply unreal.

So he tried the university within the university—the open seminar, the rap session, the "free university." He didn't learn much there either except that a lot of young men and women very much like himself were looking for something there—some direct, eye-to-eye interchange with the faculty, some answers to some deeply troubling questions. And they all wore their hair long and they all wore beads and they talked among

each other. Sure, he learned something—*from them*. He
learned that there were a great many things wrong and out
of kilter, but that no one had much of a plan to do anything
about it. But, dammit, something had to be done. He learned
that the university was tightly structured, that it had eleven
hundred and twelve rules which were constructed to guide
him to a B.A., that it was hugely impersonal, and that its
professors were a strange, impatient breed, preoccupied by
many occult things but rarely by anything that seemed *really*
to matter. He had the feeling that if he could only sit down
and talk to them, they *did* have some answers—they *were*
human and concerned. But it was only a feeling. He rarely,
if ever, got a chance to substantiate it.

He turned increasingly to the young bearded instructor who
taught a non-class on the lawn or in his back yard. Like
everyone else he tried pot. He read a lot, but very little of
it tied into anything else. His real comfort he found among
his own kind and he began to think of himself as being part
of a kind of "subculture." There were ideas there, all right,
among his own kind, in the subculture, ideas fermenting and
boiling all around. Hadn't he come to the university for ideas?
Hadn't he come to listen and ask? So the university wasn't
what his father thought it was. He couldn't explain that to
his father.

Yet his father was no fool. The son found it hard to answer
the hostile questions. Others did it. Others got their education—and they didn't turn sour and take on the look of a
chimpanzee. They got out and got good jobs. How come he,
the son, couldn't cut it?

The son answered, "Because those kind go along." They
close their eyes and play the grades game. They are cynics.
All they care about is themselves. But you couldn't go

through life blindly and caring only for yourself. You couldn't go through life and raise no voice and no fist against poverty amidst plenty, against the arrogant polluters of the earth and the air, against racism and bigotry.

So there they were face to face, stalemated and hostile. And it simply cannot be said that the university played no role in this matter. It played a very basic role. A good many of them have admitted it.

President Robert Goheen of Princeton recently pointed to the need for sweeping out educational cobwebs and said wishfully, "if the activists will let us have time to work on that." Fred M. Hechinger, Education Editor for *The New York Times,* remarked that the universities were "flirting with self-ruin." In the years since Berkeley, says Hechinger, "the original emphasis on educational reform has been brushed aside. . . . Faculty members, who tend to be more activist about the flaws of society than the deficiencies in their own departments, tend to give in to students' political demands more eagerly than to a reappraisal of education."

Kingman Brewster, Yale's prestigious president, says that the university must "simultaneously respond to those students who are so bright that they are bored with the standard academic menu, and with the greater number who are ill prepared for the new opportunity for higher education."

Clark Kerr, formerly President of the University of California, refers to "the [faculty] neglect of the undergraduate in favor of the graduate students, research, and external service," and he adds, "If they [the students] meet constantly with frustration, the answer for some of them is to escalate the tactics." And again, ". . . lack of faculty concern for teaching, endless rules and requirements, and impersonality are the inciting causes." Or take Mario Savio, Kerr's articulate student *bête noire,* who referred to the University of California as a "knowledge factory" where "nobody knows my name," and where "the operation of the machine becomes so odious you've got to stop it."

Faculty attitudes, impersonality and the mechanized, compartmentalized education are far from the only cause of student unrest. But let it be said that they are an important part of it and that they exacerbate deeper moral and political issues. And let it be said that if the "waiting-doubting student" should take a long look at himself in the mirror before he picks up a rock, a faculty member should be looking intently over his shoulder—not at the image of the student, but at himself.

A further word must be said about the young, bearded assistant professor with the "seminar" in his back yard to whom the disturbed and eager student turns in his frustration. Frustration is not always assuaged by talking to one equally frustrated. Very often the young professor (having just been a student) is as frustrated as the student who seeks him out, and, aside from the "rap sessions" he holds in his back yard, has no more idea than the student of how to handle it. If, today, this instructor or assistant professor is frustrated, wait until tomorrow—for there is a very ominous cloud on the rim of the sky.

The *New Republic* recently ran an article entitled "Academic Recession." But there is more than a recession, there is a deep academic depression—and there is every reason to believe that it is long-term.

At the mid-winter convention of the Modern Language Association, more than one thousand job applicants never got near an interviewer. When a state college in Northern California advertised for two political science positions, they received four hundred applications. Seven hundred and fifty applicants turned up for one job in the English Department at a small West Coast college. At the meeting of the American Historical Association this year, there were two thousand persons scrambling for four hundred jobs.

As one job-seeker put it, "Eight years of reading yourself blind to get a Ph.D. and if you are lucky you can beat out forty-five other poor slobs for a job that pays less than a truck driver makes."

AAUP figures show that since 1965 the economic position of college professors has slipped relative to the total population. Just in 1968 and 1969 alone, faculty compensation rose 7.2 percent compared with 8.0 percent for the labor force as a whole. In many schools in 1969–70, that had slipped to 4 percent.

Whatever the Ph.D. may in actuality be, it is the result of protracted labor on a very intensive basis and it is very expensive. The bitterness of a young Ph.D. from Harvard finding himself teaching high school is apt to be substantial. It is also apt to be communicated to his students. The same may be said for the Ph.D. from Berkeley who finds himself an instructor at Potawatomie Junior College.

Worse still is the fact that the world of higher education has been rigidified by all this. The frustrated young professor can't leave his job for another because there are no others. This "safety valve" is gone and so he festers where he is. And "festering" among young faculty on America's campus today is bad enough already.

Precisely at this time, college and university budgets are being cut and trimmed so that they are not hiring new staff. Since students continue to pour into the universities, this means two things to the new faculty member. He will not be promoted because those above him are sitting tight. More significantly, his teaching load will increase. In most schools it is already far too heavy. Even before this "depression" arrived in full force (between 1964 and 1968) there was a 47 percent increase in college enrollment and only a 35 percent increase in instructional staff. Student-faculty ratio jumped from 12.8 students per instructor to 14.0. This gap, according to all projections, will widen with great speed in the near future.

Precisely, then, when we should be reducing the ratio between student and teacher, we are drastically increasing it. Hence, precisely when we should be reducing the tensions and frustrations of the younger faculty, we are increasing them. This affects the student deleteriously in two ways: He finds it even harder to "get at" his professor and when he does he often finds a young Ph.D. festering with his own impotence and frustrations.

There probably is no solution except to "wait out" the depression. But there assuredly are palliatives, and we had damn well better start employing them. The tenured full professor has the key to most of them. He is suffering less than those in the lesser ranks. Beyond tenure, he has the lightest teaching load. The first thing the upper rank can do is to redistribute the load by taking on lower division survey courses, by giving the instructors and assistant professors a priority on summer school teaching (which increases the income); by assuming a far more active role in counseling and advising students.

All of which is merely to say that tenured full professors can pay more attention to students. In order to do so they will have to spend more time on campus than they are accustomed to; they will have to hold longer office hours; they will have to do less research and writing; they will have to give up the perquisite of summer school. All in all "professing" will become somewhat more arduous and a little less profitable. But to do *nothing* as an alternative? That may prove in the long run to be a very grim alternative indeed.

Chapter 9

A Conservative with a Radical Heart

YEARS ago I called myself a conservative. Though my father was an active Democrat, an ardent supporter of the New Deal, and a liberal in the classic sense of the word (he had great faith in the institutions of the federal system to right wrongs and to act in the best interests of all of the people), somewhere along the line, I think in my middle teens, I came to disbelieve it. My disbelief originated in looking around me.

I was, as the young are, idealistic, and one of the causes of my disillusionment was a tour for high school students of the state prison and the state hospital for the insane. I was profoundly shocked. Both institutions were old, both were understaffed, both were filthy and both were filled to overflowing with masses of human beings, infinitely miserable, less well treated than animals in zoos.

There were other factors in my departure from my father's optimistic, almost ebullient faith in the power of federal institutions to cure our ills.

Along the tracks on the north side of town there was a shantytown of considerable size. For some reason, I devel-

138

oped a friendship with a man who iived there—an unusual man with the unusual name of Barkenbust. I was fourteen, the year was 1934, and Mr. Barkenbust, as it turned out, was sixty, with an M.A. in English, and he was, needless to say, unemployed. Through Mr. Barkenbust and an equally impressive man I knew only as Sam, I was introduced to Shantytown.

Vaguely, I think, before that I had passed by Shantytown, considered that bums, after all, were bums and bums moved around and built temporary shanties along railroad tracks— shacks made of rusty old pieces of tin, scraps of lumber and canvas. And that was that.

Periodically, "bums" came to our back door for handouts, always offering to work for the food. My mother always had them split some wood and fed them on the back porch. And I still remember the song, "Hallelujah, I'm a bum/Hallelujah, I'm a bum/Hallelujah, give us a handout and revive us again." Other verses still stick in my mind, "Oh I went to the door and I asked for some bread/And the lady said bum, bum, the baker is dead." Or, "I went to the house and I knocked on the door/And the lady said bum, bum, you've been here before."

But the people in Shantytown weren't bums. They were hungry. They were transient work-hunters, they were in deep trouble, but they were not there by choice. As Mr. Barkenbust took me around, I learned a great deal about the inhabitants (some of whom were semi-permanent, having given up the "rods" in search of nonexistent better conditions elsewhere). Most of them were thoroughly decent people caught in a cataclysm.

I spent long hours asking my father about these things. Why the prison? Why the state hospital? Well, those were state matters, not federal. Why Shantytown? Why Mr. Barkenbust? Well, *no* government could provide employment in time of depression for everyone. But Mr. Roosevelt was trying. There were programs under way. But why the prison and the hospital? What was the matter with *state* government? Well, the money simply wasn't there. Same for the city.

But then, as for today's youth, somehow the answers were not enough. It couldn't be simply money. Something else was deeply wrong. Something was terribly out of joint.

As it happened, my father, who was a lawyer, regularly represented clients as a lobbyist at the state legislature—and usually I left school for extended weeks during those two months every other year and went with him. I spent hours in the gallery watching and listening and I spent hours in the corridors outside the house and senate chambers, watching and listening. Somehow, somewhere along the line, I came to think of myself as a conservative, very simplistically. I thought, here is where they can do something about the prison; here they can tackle the state hospital problem; here they face the shame and horror of the state school for the feeble-minded. And Shantytown and all the Mr. Barkenbusts are *here,* not in Washington, D.C. I became, in effect, a states' rightist and that, after all, was a conservative stance. So, in my early twenties I thought of and spoke of myself as a conservative.

And by that time I had added to the list of rank and festering local injustices, countless others. The giant Anaconda Company literally ran the state. It owned most of the daily newspapers in the state, and they were abominations of twisted journalistic never-never-land nonsense. They were not merely dull, they acted not in the interest of fact and truth, but only in the interest of one huge corporation. And every time the *Daily Missoulian* thumped on the front porch, my gorge had risen before I unfolded it—and rose higher as I read.

Miners' consumption afflicted a high percentage of the miners in Butte, yet in session after session of the legislature, dating back at least forty years, Company lobbyists had killed "silicosis" bills, which would have forced the Company to share the cost of caring for consumptive miners. The result was that some five-eights of all the welfare money raised by general taxation in Montana went to Silver Bow County (Butte).

Over the years the arrogant and open, often contemptuous control of the legislature by the Company caused me to clench my fists in fury. And that pernicious influence, via the press, spread itself into every corner of the state. Many, many others felt as I did, but aside from listing the injustices and relating to each other new stories of corruption and degradation, we felt entirely impotent.

World War II ended all that. The "cabal" which we had, in fact, become (young students, deeply frustrated, trying to evolve some kind of machinery to right wrongs and cure ills) were drafted and went off to war. Most of the "cabal" never returned to Montana. They settled where it was less infuriating to live. But a few of us, including myself, returned—pulled by the mountains, by the beauty of the place, and by some vague sense of homesickness.

Because I had gone to graduate school in California, I did not return until 1951. I was thirty-one and had a Ph.D., and I came back as Director of the State Historical Society, an agency of the state. I came back still calling myself a conservative, and I came back determined to live with what I could not change, determined to "get along," make up for lost time and enjoy the magnificent country. But it did not work out that way.

First of all, all the old injustices (except Shantytown) were unchanged. I dealt biennially with a legislature still acting first in the interest of a copper company and then in the interest of lesser special interests, but never in the interests of the indigent, the sick, the poor, the Indians (36,000 Montana Indians had an average annual income of less than $1,000) or the gross inequities which characterized the tax structure.

The prison was worse, now boasting "the hole," a dark steaming hot, cement-lined hell into which a recalcitrant prisoner was lowered. (A prisoner was to die there a few years hence.) Shortly after I had returned, a prison riot killed two prisoners and a guard. But no reforms were suggested. The state hospital was little better. The newspapers were the same—which is to say, sodden caricatures of newspapers, devoid not merely of news but devoid even of intelligent comment on any of the ills of the cities in which they were published.

A few of the members of the old "cabal" were back. Now they were young lawyers, instructors or assistant professors, priests or young men just starting businesses. Occasionally we gathered, compared notes and glumly discussed what might be done. There was the political route, but in view of Anaconda's tight control of Montana politics, that avenue seemed closed. Still, it was worth a try. Discouraging as the whole operation was, by 1956 we had elected five members of our group to the legislature. They were essentially helpless and without influence, but they were there.

Gradually we settled on a more pragmatic approach. Because we felt that a free press was the beginning place of reform, somehow we had to start a publication. We felt that nothing could be done unless we could somehow reach the public with accurate information about the ills of the community. Even pooling our limited resources, however, we could not buy the lowliest, most remote country newspaper. And even had we been able to, our circulation would have been confined to one county, and one of the lesser populated counties at that.

So we settled on a quarterly magazine. Again, pooling our resources, we launched *Montana Opinion*. The first issue, twenty-eight pages, appeared in June, 1956. In it, a young lawyer, John M. Schiltz, who had meticulously researched his subject, traced the history of "Montana's Captive Press," and carefully documented its deadening influence with examples of viciously slanted stories, the total "black-out" on liberal political candidates, and the press's complete failure to cover any news worthy of note which might discredit the Company or any of its numerous allied enterprises.

Another young lawyer, James Felt, a tax expert, slashed into the inequities and absurdities of the state's tax structure. In subsequent issues, still another lawyer, John T. Vance, who surreptitiously managed to interview prisoners at the state prison, wrote a compelling exposé on the brutality there and painted a carefully documented picture of life in prison, which went beyond the point of shock and into the realm of deep nausea. Three weeks later, when a riot which we had clearly forecast actually occurred at the prison, several high state officials pointedly remarked that we had, in fact, incited the riot.

Montana Opinions never had a circulation which exceeded 800. It ran for only four issues and then we were broke. But we did manage an exposé of Company lobbying methods, a detailed analysis of the hypocrisy of the candidates for high state office in the year 1956, a view of corruption and payoffs from the point of view of an "independent" running for the legislature, an attack on the methods of school financing, and we managed to prod several sacred cows.

How much influence did we have? It is difficult to assess. The Company press had been under attack by journalists outside Montana for many years (*The Nation, Harper's, The Denver Post,* Gunther's *Inside USA,* etc.), but within a year of Schiltz's *Montana Opinion* exposé, the Company sold all its newspapers to the independent Lee chain.

Though collector's items today, and though its circulation was minuscule, one might guess from the number of times *Montana Opinion* articles have been reprinted, used and quoted from in the years since, that its impact was greater than the brevity of its life and its meager circulation would imply. Prison reforms *were* instituted in 1957; the tax structure *was* studied and somewhat overhauled; a bill *was* passed that required lobbyists to register as lobbyists—a very minor reform.

The "cabal," as such, broke up, each of us enduring a certain raised-eyebrow response from "responsible" people. As for myself, two members of the Board of Trustees of the Historical Society (both of them in their cups, presumably because they had fortified themselves for the encounter) came to my house rather late one evening to inform me that I must either quit my association with *Montana Opinion* or quit as director of the Society. When I pointed out that it was academic because we had just folded due to lack of funds, they appeared relieved. When I pointed out, further, that it was done on my own time as a private citizen, they remained silent; but when I pointed out that it did not seem to me that I was endangering them anyhow since I was a "conservative," one of them focused on me intently for a moment and said, "Toole, if you are a conser'ative, you are a conservative with a damned radical heart." And I have never called myself a conservative since.

And still, it was not enough. I kept looking around me at all that was wrong and dirty and ignored, and I felt like Leslie Fiedler, who had written (in *Montana Opinion* at that—he wasn't quite as famous a critic then as now), "It is vexing to have to say it, but I might as well make it clear that it is only because I like Montana, after all, that I consider it worth raising my voice over its more flagrant weaknesses. . . . because in the beauty of its natural setting, man, when he is vile (and when is he not?) seems viler than elsewhere."

And so I wrote a book. It was called *Montana: An Uncommon Land*. I did not really intend it to be a savage book—and indeed, in 1970 (it was published in 1957), it does not seem even mildly savage. Yet it seemed so then to a surprisingly large number of Montanans. Why did I have to concentrate on what was wrong when there was so much that was right? If I loved the state, how could I abuse it so? If I felt that way, why didn't I leave? Well, I did.

I did not leave because I wanted to, but because I had to. I was not fired, although I believe I would have been. It was simply that I was sufficiently frustrated so that I felt myself becoming ineffective. I found myself doing things that I *knew* amounted to spinning wheels.

For example, the Society published a historical quarterly of which I was the editor. At one particularly frustrating period, I wrote an editorial which was very unhistorical. The legislature was then in session and it was its usual self. I wrote an editorial on its activities in which, among other hard things, I said that the session was full of "pusillanimous slobs."

Several legislators demanded that I be fired then and there, but it was late in the session and they didn't get around to it. It was a foolishly explosive thing to do, and there was no real purpose behind it. And I think I knew then and there that I would leave. And I would leave because I could not abide the snail's pace of reform when the problems were so obvious, the pain so painful and the alleviation, when it came at all, was so piecemeal and so meager.

So I left and went to New York and other places—and I left not as a conservative and not as a liberal in the eyes of the Montana establishment, but as a *radical*—and an unstable one, at that.

Now this little autobiographical sketch is by way of saying something not only about why I feel the way I do concerning today's crisis on the campus, but a little more. I am amused rather than amazed that in the light of my recent writings on the subject, a number of people who have formerly considered me an air-headed radical have now clasped me to their bosoms as a right-of-center and damned sound conservative concerning student disruptions. The editor of the *Billings Gazette,* whose reprinting of my initial letter to my brother started the whole ruckus, and who has known me for some years, recently advised his readers editorially, you had better go back and read the earlier Toole. It will be enlightening.

A young physics professor, David Rudnik, from UCLA, with whom I appeared on the "Life with Linkletter" show recently, read from the first section of a very short book I had written on campus violence, then read from the second section, then looked up and asked quizzically, "Which is the real Professor Toole, the one who is against the students or the one who is for them?" A very good question, which I had neither the time nor the inclination to answer. But I do now.

In light of my own experiences very sketchily outlined above, and in spite of the very hard things I have said about students and the younger generation in the preceding pages, I feel an immediate, quick and very powerful sympathy for student dissent on American campuses today. It has been built into me by my years both on and off campuses.

When I came back to Montana, things had changed vastly—and for the better. But still, everywhere, we move so slowly, so timorously, with too little and too late into the battle against the things we have to fight to survive. The trouble is that I *do* understand their frustrations and their anger. And I understand their disgust for hypocrisy and their despair when *my* generation says, "If you don't love it, leave it."

I understand it because, in a different way and at a different time, it was said to me—again and again—and somehow I could not explain to those who said it, "But it is precisely because I love it that I dissent and criticize it." It is not sufficient to love a place blindly, a state or a nation. It is only sufficient to love it with your eyes wide open and often with your fists clenched.

Some years ago William Faulkner came to a summer writers' conference and rather mumbled and stumbled his way through a talk on how to write a novel. A woman in the audience rose and said, "Don't you think that so-and-so will some day write a great novel about Montana because he loves the state so?" Faulkner replied, "But, madam, in order to write well about a place, you have to hate it." And then he added thoughtfully, "the way a man hates his wife."

The aphorism "Love it or leave it" decaled on so many car bumpers and windows today implies that if you love anything about something you must love everything. But if you *really* love your country, you must detest its cancers—for they will kill it. And you must not just stand there and detest the cancers, you must take action. First you must discover and point out that they are there, then you must get a very careful diagnosis, and then you must prescribe the cure. You cannot love what is detestable and must not love what kills love itself.

My cavil with the younger generation is not that they dissent, not that they are impatient, not that they feel a terrible urgency and express it. My argument is that they must maintain what they love by the most efficacious means at hand. They must not be so blinded by the ills that beset us that they kill what they love in the process of exorcising what they hate.

I feel a spontaneous sympathy for the dissenters and the deeply concerned young for another reason which a great majority of my generation seem to overlook. And we cannot afford to overlook it any longer. There is something very vital which the young *do* understand and which we do *not*.

Early in this book I said that time accelerates, that it feeds on our choices, that it pushes us as individuals inexorably and ever more swiftly. What I did not say is that it does the same thing on a broader and deeper scale to peoples and nations.

While the young, it seems to me, do not recognize the swift diminution of their opportunities in their own personal lives (one has to live that), they seem to me to have an almost uncanny understanding of today's deepening acceleration of time. Because they are brighter or more observant than their elders? I think not. It is because my generation, bearing its years and its scars and its accomplishments, finds it impossible to believe that we are actually living in a time of "revolution"—not merely a slightly accelerated evolution. We are not living in a revolutionary period launched and sustained by the New Left or any other revolutionary group, but rather one attributable to the fact that the *velocity* of everything (social, economic, moral, technological, political and religious) has swung us beyond that point of ready reference to many of the old guidelines and immutabilities.

I do not mean to say that we have swung (yet) completely out of our own history, but that we have bulged beyond that point where a good many common guidelines of doing business, getting and spending, working and playing, have efficacy. And we have not yet evolved new ones.

When I was twenty, frustrated, angry, and reformist oriented as I was, those guidelines *were* there. My trouble was in learning to use them, to break into the open with some running room. My dissent was not based on a feeling that time was critically short, but rather that reform was absurdly slow. I had no sense that we would simply run out of time. Today's twenty-year-old *has* that sense of urgency—and he is right.

Moreover, I grew up under national administrations (the New Deal) that were clearly reformist and experimental. Today's twenty-year-old not only recognizes that a state of crisis exists and that many guidlines are ineffective (with time running out), but he sees a national administration not only conducting business as usual, but moving at a pace in all areas of endeavor that would admirably have suited the

1920's, but is frighteningly anachronistic in 1970. So his sense of frustration is greatly compounded by a sense of urgency.

Arthur Schlesinger, Jr. refers to this revolution (which he does not call it) as "the velocity of history" and notes that one of its hallmarks is "the conviction of personal power-lessness, the sense of being beset, beleaguered and persecuted. It extends not only to Black Panthers and members of the Students for a Democratic Society, but also to businessmen, publishers, generals and (as we have recently come to observe) Vice Presidents."

And so it does. But mostly it afflicts the young because, unlike their elders, they see that we must act quickly to establish new responses; we must establish new and powerful coalitions among ourselves and fill the swiftly gathering vacuum with new affirmations to support old American ideals. Thus with their state of mind and with this sense of urgency and dismay, I sympathize deeply. But I would add two hundred words of caution:

I will grant you your crisis and grant what it implies and grant you that we must act and change and redesign. But what is happening is not a series of demonstrations of our decay, but, in the long run, is rather the price of our progress. If you will act (however swiftly), positively rather than negatively, I and any number of my kind will join you with glad hearts. But if you see this crisis as the symptoms of a disease which crop to the surface from a core of rottenness in the heart of America, we will neither join you nor will you succeed—because you will then be trying to cure an illness which is not fatal with an antidote of massive poison.

Chapter 10

How to Go About It

So the channels are plugged? We cannot make our voices heard? How do we change things then? In the first place, the channels are *not* plugged, but they are not so easily employed as might at first seem to be the case. For one thing, as Churchill put it, "Democracy is the worst form of government ever invented—except for every other." In the second place, it works not only within a complicated structure of checks and balances, but this, in turn, works only within the generalized principle of compromise.

Often the channels *seem* plugged, the wires of communication *seem* cut because the young do not recognize a channel or a wire when they see one. I was flying with a friend of mine in a light plane a few months ago and I was enthralled with our "communications" via radio with sundry stations along the route. No matter how I moved the earphones around, all I could make of the ground-to-air and air-to-ground conversation was a series of cracklings, beeps and tones interspersed with faint, flat voices. Yet the pilot, with earphones identical to mine, had no difficulty in understanding

and being understood at all. This, of course, comes from practice, from knowing what the beeps mean and from a tuning
of the ear to faint, flat voices from the ground. You do not
learn that in a day.

The first and most significant power available to the young
is political. That they are disillusioned with politics, that the
defeat, for example, of Eugene McCarthy was a severe shock
to them does not alter one whit the fact that the potential
political power of the young is very great indeed. In the first
place, it is great in absolute numbers. Of the total number
of registered voters (120,000,000), 31,000,000 are under
thirty (more than one-fourth) and 11,000,000 will be added
when the voting age drops to eighteen. I say "when" rather
than "if" because even should the Supreme Court negate the
recent Congressional act giving the vote to eighteen-year-olds,
states can still give the eighteen-year-olds the vote—and it
will come. So now we are talking about more than one-third
of the American voters being under thirty.

In the election of 1968, for example, Nixon won with 43.4
percent of the vote. Humphrey had 42.7 percent, which means
that Nixon's plurality was .7 percent. Those 42,000,000
voters under thirty, therefore, assume an even greater posture
of power.

It has always amazed me that the ardent young supporters
of Eugene McCarthy, almost all of them, expressed bitter
disillusionment with the political process after his defeat.

There is, so far as I know, no precedent in American history for what happened in that election. In effect, the young
and ardent campaigners and voters were instrumental in the
resignation of an incumbent President of the United States.
The fact that Richard Nixon ultimately won that election
should not obscure the startling demonstration by the young

of a very great political punch. Yet it did and does obscure that fact.

This, once again, is due to a lack of knowledge by the young of the political process. Instead of holding on and welding themselves together in the name and principle of an ideal, instead of *using* the defeat of McCarthy to build a coalition and to add to their power, they disintegrated in disillusionment. Nor can a member of my generation entirely escape the familiar "nowness" of this disillusionment, "If we can't win *now,* we won't play."

Naïveté is not the father of disillusionment. It is more often the father of growth. But that requires a certain tenacity and toughness—which are two of the basic ingredients in the formula for successful political action. The young activists must understand that fact if they are to employ the most powerful tool they have with maximum effect.

They must understand some other political facts of life (which the majority, in my opinion, do not). The most powerful political movements in America (and for that matter in most democracies) have usually had an "ideal" at the far end. In other words, however pragmatic the "means," the goal is an "ideal"—a probably unattainable something, but very much and very powerfully a something. So you get Jefferson and the vision of the independent man close to the soil; you get Andrew Jackson and the ideal of restoring opportunity to the "common man"; you get Theodore Roosevelt and "The New Nationalism"; Woodrow Wilson and "The New Freedom"; Franklin Roosevelt and "The New Deal"; and John F. Kennedy and "The New Frontier."

Now none of these "ideals" was truly reached; all arose from a need for reform and in response to serious national ills. Many of the young today *should* remember (even if they read no history) the spirit, the *élan,* the ebullience of the Kennedy era, short as it was.

In terms of disillusionment and the trauma of failure, let the young activists remember this: Most third party or third "force" movements in American history have "failed," from the Farmers Alliance, through the Populists to the Progressive Party. But those "failures" were failures only in terms of "nowness." In 1924 Robert LaFollette was badly defeated as presidential candidate under the flag of the Progressive Party. He carried only one state and received only thirteen electoral votes. Yet by 1932, almost all of the planks in the Progressive Party's platform had been adopted.

Oddly enough, the last "third force" movement, "McCarthyism," in spite of McCarthy's defeat, had more "now" effects than any other preceding movement. The young college students who rang doorbells from Maine to California were not only instrumental in bringing about Lyndon Johnson's retirement, they fundamentally changed American foreign policy. All the more reason for puzzlement, and all the more reason for them to reappraise their political power. All the less reason for them to assert that "we cannot make our voices heard" and slink off in dissarray with the assertion that the political process doesn't work. All the less reason for Linda Eldridge to moan that she emerged from a political "defeat," saying, "We worked our hearts out for him and had them broken. And hardened."

If at the end of most successful political movements there stands an "ideal," so progress toward it depends on pragmatism. So, between the end of all hunger in America and the attainment of that goal, stands work at the ward and precinct level, stand long and tedious hours of work in legislative corridors and the halls of Congress. So between the ideal and the attainment, stand disappointment and bills that never get out of committee. And between the goal and the reaching of it stand compromise, hard trades, twelve thousand hours of bargaining, sixteen thousand hours of raising money for candidates who share the ideal, and countless hours of study.

The mood of a nation often changes rapidly. But that is an illusion. Only the point of "break-over" is rapid. Behind that change itself lies the tough, tenacious, informed and dedicated reformer. And the compromise.

The word *elite,* like a great many others in today's political lexicon, has taken on connotations which never originally attached to it. Once it simply meant "the choice part of or flower (of society, etc.)." Today it and its offspring *elitist* mean a good deal more. Not merely does elite mean aristocracy, it means the carefully developed intellectual few. It implies not only exclusivity but "best" in intellectual respects.

Can the "elite" compromise? No, because compromise can only mean to an elite that the process would reduce their elitism which is the essence of what they are.

Are many of today's student militants "elitist"? Indeed they are, and one has only to listen to them to discover it. Nothing irritates them more than to be termed "elitist," but that does not alter the fact that they are. When you are right and you have all the answers, compromise becomes an exercise in intellectual degradation.

In the primer of how to *use* politics, therefore, one might begin with the assertion that compromise is an essential ingredient of the political process and is therefore non-elitist. One might grant, I think, that Winston Churchill had a superior intellect, that he compromised constantly and that neither his integrity nor his intellect suffered much degradation in the process. Throw in Jefferson and a few hundred others whose elitism never got in the way of actual intellect and view their accomplishments. At least in this one view of politics as power (and what else is it?) one might say to the militant student under the rubric of "How to Go About it": First of all, stop being elitist. It may hurt your ego; it won't damage your brain.

Pragmatism. It, too, was once a word with a few simple meanings: "(1) matter-of-fact treatment of things; (2) the doctrine that the whole meaning of a conception expresses itself in practical consequences." But today it has other connotations, the most pernicious of which is that pragmatism precludes idealism. The fact is that they can live very comfortably in the same house—and that in the sound political structure, they *must* live together.

It may be that the error here (in young minds) lies in the incompatibility of the two *philosophies,* the one propounded by Royce, the other by James. But politics is not philosophy. So in the primer of how to go about things politically, one might say to the dissident student: Keep the ideal (which is the end), but develop some pragmatism (which is the means).

A pragmatist, for instance, would recognize at once that violence on the left produces strength on the right. His *ideal,* a better, freer, more joyful life, can only be ill served by the employment of the wrong means. A pragmatist would recognize another vital thing: that the progressive alienation of "liberals" from the cause, an alienation inherent in the expression of absolutism of any kind, will lose him a possible coalition which may in the end prove imperative.

The success of the political process, the maximum utilization of the political power which the young *do* have, depends further on the crystal clarity of goals. I do not think this is necessarily true in European politics, especially French and Italian. It *is* true of American politics because in the political realm, as in every other, the American people are "goal-oriented." They always have been; there is little indication that this has changed. The political party, as such, is simply not a goal. It is important for the young American to realize that the increasing numbers of "independent" voters in America (a trend obviously destined to continue) is a manifestation of goal orientation. People will increasingly cross party lines with nary a twinge of conscience, because their eye is on the goal, not the party.

Political platforms, of course, do not really express goals at all. They should be classified simply under the general heading of "The Games People Play." But actual goals remain vital.

So the third rule in the primer for young activists who seek to use political channels to reform America, should be this: Stop talking in generalities, i.e., the "quality of life," "participatory democracy," "power to the people," "a new life style," and do some hard homework.

We seek an end to poverty and hunger in America. Given our GNP, positing the end of the Vietnam War, and positing our present tax level, by what specific means, agencies and statutes can we guarantee that, of the 55 billion dollars a year now being spent in Vietnam, 58.8 percent will be reinvested in direct aid to the poverty-striken and only 41.2 percent will revert to the Pentagon?

Says the purist, goddam, 100 percent must revert to the poverty program! Says the pragmatist, nobody will go for that, but we have a fair chance on 58.8 percent. And this is the *specific* legislation which will be required to do it and this is the *specific* reshuffling of boards, commissions and bureaus which will have to be brought about if it is to work. Knowing that bureaus, boards and commissions "eat up" vast quantities of this money just to maintain themselves, we must create a governmental machine which will perform this function for 12 percent of the monies available.

The goal, freedom from poverty and hunger, simply cannot be reached by asserting that we are a wealthy country and that poverty must go. It can only be reached by hard study based on hard planning and meticulous information—all employed in the cold light of the knowledge that enormously powerful pressure groups will oppose the plan and that government, wittingly or otherwise, will itself constitute the chief pressure group. Impossible? No—simply very difficult.

Ralph Nader, even before he was assisted by the "raiders," shook up and even won a one-man battle with the largest corporation extant by an attack based on incontrovertible evidence and abundant fact. He has repeatedly shaken other corporations and the government itself with charges based on fact and solutions based on meticulous research. He is living proof that it can be done. He is also living proof that rhetoric and generalities did not do it; hard work, tenacity and specific goals did it. He has not, of course, reformed America. But what if there were 3,000 Naders and 15,000 "raiders"?

So, young dissident, study very hard how to *specify* your goals and study very hard how you get there *specifically*—and then go raiding. Do not take any generalities in your baggage and burden your tongue with no fiery rhetoric. It is an exercise in complete futility to advocate the destruction of what exists if you have nothing but empty words to put in its place.

It is equally futile to say "We must change," and then be unprepared to answer very specifically the question, "How?"

To an extent, I think I would go along with John Galbraith's view of the American economic system, that the free marketplace does *not* determine what happens; that supply and demand function only in the vaguest kind of way, and that the consumer does *not,* in fact, determine what he consumes. The producer creates a desire for an unnecessary product with enormous influence via the media and then sells unneeded products to unneedful consumers.

But one can be "Galbraithian" and still assert that the consumers (in this case, the young consumers) *could* have enormous economic power if they chose, simply because they constitute an enormous and wealthy market. Numerous studies of the buying power of the teen-ager have been made and it is unnecessary to belabor the point. Indeed, in many instances they *create* new styles, new music, new literature which amounts to billions when converted into sales.

That the young have been miserably exploited, not only by my generation, but ironically, by their own, needs no documentation. The evidence is overwhelming. In music, for instance, only the Beatles and a few other rock groups made what might be called music. The consequent rock movement with its innumerable by-products in style was, for a while, highly creative, individual and splendidly experimental. With appalling speed, the entire movement, the entire "thing" was taken over (most often by young and very cynical English entrepreneurs) by those who mechanized un-talent, un-music, and un-style into cheap, non-individual, non-experimental junk. In the process they got very, very rich.

That is a *negative* example of the potential economic power of the young. Suppose that that power, solely on the economic basis, were to be used positively? Suppose, instead of talking about environmental degradation, the young consumer used very well-planned and selectively determined boycotts? For instance, We will buy no beer, but will make our own until the beer industry comes up with disposable containers or returnable bottles. Suppose the young were to say, We will buy no leaded gasoline until Detroit designs engines with lower compression? Suppose the young said, We will not buy (and we will dissuade our parents from buying) all detergents? We will launch a national "back to soap" movement until the industry removes all phosphates and other pollutants from its products.

Suppose the young across the nation had joined one lonely, fawn-eyed man named Cesar Chavez and lent their enormous influence to the boycott on grapes? I doubt that there would today be a single migrant grape-picker working for less than the minimum national hourly wage.

The boycott, the consumer's strike, is no panacea. Its success depends on meticulous organization and, again, on hard work and tenacity. Yet it is a powerful and effective weapon which the young have rarely used.

They flexed their muscles as "freedom riders" in the South just for a fleeting moment—and gave hope to a million blacks. They *can* organize. But can they stay organized and stay with it?

Young Americans from every state in the Union, to the tune of from 25,000 to 460,000, will travel across America, endure rain, mud, hunger, cold and deprivation to attend a rock festival. Think what an impact they would have if they showed up in such numbers in the Florida orange groves to help the migrant workers pick oranges, donating what they picked to the workers' meager pay. Could the giant citrus fruit companies (Coca-Cola is one of the largest) any longer hide the horror of the migrant worker's life from a shocked America? I think not. Could the owners deny that in violation of state and federal law, child labor among migrant workers is the order of the day?

If the young were refused in their efforts to help the migrants, would not the reflection cast on the giant citrus industry nevertheless reveal their exploitation of human beings and callous disregard of sanitary and other minimal worker facilities? Could they maintain the shameful system under the bright gaze of 3,000 youngsters and TV's unblinking eye? I do not believe they could.

The Woodstock Rock Festival was thoroughly covered by television. There were more than 400,000 young men and women there from all over America. In spite of cold, rain and mud, they were having a ball. I remember thinking, my God, what a power *that* would be turned to a helpful cause. What a power that would be if, instead of gathering in a muddy pasture, they gathered in a ghetto with hammers and nails, rat poison and scrub brushes and a million bottles of one-a-day vitamins. What a power *that* would be in a thousand different places and in the interests of a hundred different causes ranging from ghettos to Indian reservations, from dirty streets to filthy beaches, and in the halls of Congress.

But I thought then, and think now, these are the people who shout "now"; these are the people who cry for "action" to set right the ills of America. They are gathered in this pasture 400,000 strong. I wondered then and wonder now if any of them saw irony in that. They were there purely and *en masse* to indulge *themselves*. If they could do that (and simply by word of mouth that spread across a nation),

then where are the channels plugged and where are the wires
cut that would prevent them from so gathering to indulge
someone *other* than themselves—the Chicanos, the hopeless
in Appalachia, the deprived in the ghetto? Once again, the
channels are *not* plugged, the wires are *not* cut. The young
simply have not seen them. What blinds them? I don't know,
but I would suggest that self-indulgence is a large part of
it. They have this great power. Will they turn it outward
to help or only inward to dissipate it? So I would say to
the activist as point number four under the heading of "How
to Go About It": If you can gather 400,000 strong at the
drop of a word because ten rock groups are going to hold
forth in a pasture in New York, you can also march to the
beat of a different drummer. Gather instead in a citrus grove
or in Watts and gather not for yourselves but for those who
need help. Not only would you help them, you would focus
the eyes of middle America on them *and* on yourselves in
a way not to alienate the majority of middle Americans but
to garner their respect and admiration.

But there are powers possessed by the young which go
beyond the political and the economic. In the last few years
this power has been surfacing and then disappearing, causing
only a ripple. It could cause a great wave. It depends on
you.

Corporate law firms have recently had a hard time recruit-
ing the brightest graduates of the best law schools. Prestigious
medical clinics have had the same problem. Corporate recruiters on campuses (at least until the recent increase in
unemployment) were finding it more difficult to attract the
best students.

Young lawyers wanted to be in a position to involve themselves in current social problems. They wanted to be in a position to defend indigent clients as well as wealthy; they wanted to tackle problems brought to them by the American Civil Liberties Union; they wanted to involve themselves in the legal problems which arise from critical social problems.

Young doctors, likewise, wanted to practice not in exclusive medical clinics with well-heeled patients, but wanted to deal with malnutrition and the diseases that arise from poverty and ghettos and skid rows.

Increasingly, young Ph.D.'s want to avoid the multiversity and choose, instead, the small schools where the student-faculty ratio will enable them to be close to their students.

Instead of asking first about salary, stock options and retirement plans, corporate recruiters have told me repeatedly that the student now asks about the company's racial policy, if it is committed to a fair quota of blacks, if it is involved in the production of war goods, and so on.

Such young, bright, professional people *could* change medical, legal and corporate conscience; they *could* turn the professions toward a vastly greater involvement in social problems and processes. In short, they *could* play a powerful role in reform.

Taken all together, the power of youth to change things through political, economic and social structures is greater today than it has ever been in the past. That so many of them cannot see that that is true is ominous.

So the fifth point in the "How to Go About It" category is perhaps a catchall upon which the others depend. You must open your eyes, look behind you and ahead of you and you must work very hard. You must understand that America *will* listen to you but that when it does you must have something concrete to say. If you find her somewhat deaf at the moment, consider that that could be due to the fact that loud noises cause deafness. Closely reasoned argument does not.

You must continue to dissent, to oppose what you believe to be wrong and to say so as often as you have to and as cogently as you can. You must be idealistic and pragmatic and very well informed. You must be tough and tenacious. None of which—none of which at all—will be worth a tinker's dam unless you see above all that America can change and change fast, with precisely the means and tools you already have at hand.

Chapter 11

The Time Has Come

Iт was Alice's walrus who said that—but doubtless even he would think of something other than cabbages and kings to talk about today.

I do not think that blunt talk and utter candor is divisive. It has become fashionable to condemn Spiro T. Agnew for attacking "the media" and sundry other groups and activities. Some say that the Vice President of the United States has no business thus unburdening himself of his beliefs. Some hold that Agnew's attack on "the media" carried an implicit threat of censorship. Following the attack, however, "the media" promptly struck back and have been at him ever since. It might be more accurate to say that Agnew was a stimulant rather than a depressant and one may disagree with his stance (as I do) and still assert that he not only had a right to say what he said but that the ensuing interchange was a good thing for the country.

I do not think that exchanges between the older and the younger generations which may sometimes grow hot are divisive. I think they are imperative. I do not think we need

165

whisper—and I am not even concerned if we shout. Obviously we should avoid *argumentum ad hominem* and rage, but candor, boldness and bluntness—so much the better.

And I think that in our dialogue we should each bear something in mind. To talk bluntly, face to face, both of us should set aside certain hindrances.

For example, for the past few years I have been working with an Indian group on our campus endeavoring to set up a Red Studies Program for Indians, much like our Black Studies Program. We were ultimately successful, but in the beginning, though I had lived in close proximity to Indian people most of my life and had a number of close Indian friends, I felt a vague sense of restraint whenever we met in solemn conclave—the whites and the Indians. It was obvious that the Indians felt that same. They were courteous but impassively constrained. Both groups were walking on eggshells and whispering. Both groups offered strategies and plans with tentative timorousness. We were getting no place.

On the white panel, there was a young, red-headed Irishman who had adopted two Indian children and who not only had a short fuse on his patience, but a shorter fuse on his temper. We had met with our Indian committee colleagues perhaps a dozen times and this day, after a few tentative interchanges, the room was so quiet all you could hear was the droning of the flies.

Suddenly my red-headed colleague, who was, in any event, given to colorful language, leaned forward and said approximately this: "Listen, you red-skinned bastards, if you think I am packing any guilt around because my forebears damaged your people, forget it. I don't give a damn about the past and I don't give a damn about what you think I am.

We are not going to get any program at all if you bastards sit there staring at us like Sitting Bull."

There was dead silence in the room for a moment. Even the flies stopped buzzing. Then a young Blackfoot leaned forward, eyeball to eyeball with the redhead, and said approximately this: 'Listen you red-headed paleface, if you think I am a damn bit worried about your guilt, forget it. Just remember Custer and remember that we will take no more bullshit from you than we did from him. We are Indians and damn proud of it."

Again the silence and then, suddenly, everyone in the room burst into laughter. Within three weeks, sometimes shouting at each other, arguing vehemently, all constraint gone, we had hammered out a Red Studies Program.

In the dialogue between the younger generation and the older, we must not carry around the conviction that if we are candid we will injure mutual sensibilities. We must not be hindered by vague senses of guilt. There should be no deference, just civility—and civility does not preclude hard words, directly and honestly delivered. We need very badly to talk to each other and listen to each other—not to win points in the game of debating, but to draw closer in an understanding why each of us feels the way he does.

The red-headed Irishman and the red-skinned Indian will never fully understand each other. Their backgrounds and the myriad moments of their different individual lives preclude that. But they can, and are, working beside each other in full understanding in that one common cause.

My brother and I, even with nearly identical backgrounds and common genes, will never fully understand each other. We love each other, but we will always disagree about a great many things—and I will never fully understand him, nor he me.

The two of us, your generation and mine, will never fully understand each other. It would be absurd if we did, because then we would be no different—and if we were not different, you and I, the world would be in a far sorrier mess than it is now. It is not only inevitable that you react differently to the times than I do, it is imperative.

But if we meet face to face, air our differences in strong language, sit across an old table from each other and reach toward each other, we can leave that room liking each other. And if we meet again and then again and reach still further, a very strange and necessary thing will happen. We will not fully understand each other, not ever, but we will begin to love each other.

We are together, you and I, on a small and dwindling planet passing through an incredibly cold and infinite blackness. And we are here briefly. It is the same journey we take. We will be separated soon enough as "time and hour run through the roughest day." What is that fine song of yours, "I Want to Hold Your Hand"?

Well, why not? It is the same journey and it is a rough one. Let us hold hands. At the root of it, we are all deeply involved in the same cause, passing through the same time, occupying the same space. The time has come for us to look out into the darkness—and then into each other's eyes.

Bibliography

FAR from being definitive, this bibliography is not even selective. These are simply the books and articles to which I referred for specific information or simply because they intrigued me and I found them enlightening. The literature on the young, the generation gap, the crises on campus runs into a tonnage which is simply appalling. It would take a full year, full time, simply to list it. The articles and books listed below are places to start—nothing more.

Adelson, Joseph, "What Generation Gap?" *The New York Times Magazine,* January 18, 1970.

Altbach, Philip G., "The Future of the American Student Movement," *Liberal Education,* Vol. 52 (October, 1966).

American Association of University Professors, Policy Documents and Reports, AAUP, 1969.

American Civil Liberties Union (booklet), "Academic Freedom and Civil Liberties of Students in Colleges and Universities," April, 1970, New York.

"At War with War," *Time,* May 18, 1970.

Barzun, Jacques, *The American University.* New York: Harper and Row, 1968.

Bickel, Alexander M., "The Tolerance of Violence on the Campus," *The New Republic,* June 13, 1970.

Boorstin, Daniel, "A Case of Hypochondria," *Newsweek,* July 6, 1970.

Brown, Michael, *The Politics and Anti-Politics of the Young. and Development in the 1970's.* New York: Praeger, 1970.

Brown, Michael, *The Politics and Anti-Politics of the Young.* Beverly Hills, California: Glencoe Press, 1969.

Chase, Margaret, "Voice of Reason: Call to the Center," *Time,* June 15, 1970.

Commager, Henry Steele, "Is Freedom Dying in America?" *Look,* July 14, 1970.

Davidson, Sara, "Open Land: Getting Back to the Communal Garden," *Harper's,* June, 1970.

Dozer, Donald Marquand, "The Deviant University," *The University Bookman,* Bristol, Conn., Autumn, 1969.

Duberman, Martin, "On Misunderstanding Student Rebels," *Atlantic Monthly,* Vol. 222 (November, 1968).

East, John P., "Why So Few Conservatives on Campus?" *Wall Street Journal,* July 2, 1970.

Eldridge, Linda, "What to Do with Our Lives?" *Time,* May 11, 1970.

Foster, Julian, and Long, Durwood, eds., *Protest: Student Activism in America.* New York: William Morrow and Co., Inc., 1970.

Genovese, Eugene D., "A Massive Breakdown," *Newsweek,* July 6, 1970.

Hacker, Andrew, *The End of the American Era.* New York: Atheneum, 1970.

Hacker, Andrew, "We Will Meet As Enemies," *Newsweek,* July 6, 1970.

Hechinger, Fred M., "Universities Flirt with Self Ruin," *The New York Times,* July 16, 1970.

Hechinger, Fred M. and Grace, *Teenage Tyranny*. Greenwich, Conn.: Fawcett Books, 1963.

Hofstadter, Richard, "The Age of Rubbish," *Newsweek,* July 6, 1970.

Hook, Sidney, "Second Thoughts on Berkeley," *Teacher's College Record,* New York, October 2, 1965.

Howe, Irving, "New Course for the New Left," *Saturday Review,* May 30, 1970.

Hunter, Shirley, *Handbook for the Hip Anti-Radicals*. Menomonie, Wisconsin: United Students for America, 1970.

Landers, Clifford E. and Cicarelli, "Academic Recession," *The New Republic,* May 9, 1970.

Lipsit, Seymour Martin, "The Banality of Revolt," *Saturday Review,* July 18, 1970.

Lipsit, Seymour Martin, and Robb, Earl, "The Non-Generation Gap," *Commentary,* August, 1970.

Lipsit, Seymour, and Wolin, Sheldon, *The Berkeley Student Revolt*. Garden City, New York: Anchor Books, 1965.

Lynd, Staughton, "Again—Don't Tread on Me," *Newsweek,* July 6, 1970.

McCully, George E., "History Begins at Home," *Saturday Review,* May, 1970.

New York Times Encyclopedic Almanac. New York: New York Times, 1970.

Okles, John F., "The University and the Unstudents," *School and Society,* October 26, 1968.

Peterson, Richard E., "The Scope of Organized Student Protest in 1964–1965." Princeton: New Jersey Educational Testing Service, 1966.

"Rise of the Dynamite Radicals," *Time,* September 7, 1970.

Rosten, Leo, "Who Speaks For the Young?" *Look,* May 19, 1970.

Schiltz, John, "Montana's Captive Press," *Montana Opinion,* June, 1956.

Schlesinger, Arthur M., Jr., "The Velocity of History," *Newsweek,* July 6, 1970.

Sternhell, Ruth Carol, "Writing on Revolution," *McCalls,* July, 1970.

Sugar, Andy, "On the Campus Firing Line with Al Capp," *Saga,* December, 1969.

Sweigert, William T., "Moral Preemption: Claims of the 'Regent' Under Positive Law." (Sweigert is U. S. District Judge, Northern District of California. Mimeographed. No publisher listed.)

"The Three Wars: at Kent State, in New Haven, in Cambodia: Issues of the UCLA Strike." Los Angeles: publisher unknown, 1970.

Tinker *vs* Des Moines Independent School District, *et al.,* 393 *vs* 503, 1969.

"What White Students Think of Black Studies," *Life,* June, 1970.

Woodring, Paul, *The Higher Learning in America: A Reassessment.* New York: McGraw-Hill, 1968.

"Youth 1967: The Challenge of Change," *The American Scholar,* Vol. 36, No. 4 (Autumn, 1967).

INDEX

academic freedom, 25, 33, 37, 38
academician, 36
activists, 133, 154
Agnew, Spiro T., 165
Alien and Sedition Act of 1798, 121
American Association of University Professors, 34, 37, 38, 135
American Civil Liberties Union, 98, 103, 163
"American Crisis," 112
American Indian War, 119, 120
American pendulum, 121
Anaconda Co., 140
anarchism, jejune, 11
anarchy, 20
anti-intellectualism, 62
Antioch, 128
anti-pollution, 52
Appalachia, 116, 162

behavioral guidelines, 20
Berkeley, 79
Bill of Rights, 99
Billings Gazette, 146
Black Death, 47
Black Panthers, 109, 150
Black Student Union, 9, 62
Black Studies Program, 166
Blackfoot, 167
Boorstin, Daniel J., 112–115

boycotts, 160
Brewster, Kingman, 133
Brown, Lester R., 88
brutality, police, 69
Burger, Warren, 108, 110

"cabal," 141–142, 144
Cambodia, 34, 37, 67
Capote, Truman, 62, 64
Capp, Al, 7
cataclysm, 19
censorship, 32
Chavez, Cesar, 160
Chicago Seven, 99
Chicanos, 162
civil and constitutional rights, 101
Cleaver, Eldridge, 109
College of San Mateo, 79
Commager, Henry Steele, 112
Commissioner of Indian Affairs, 119
commune, 14, 18, 53, 56
commune dwellers, 15, 20
Communist, 58
cooptation, 74
Custer, George Armstrong, 167

Denver Post, 144
Depression, 54
disruptive students, 98
dogmatists, doctrinaire, 31

175